D1244595

Hester

Historical Fiction about the Life of a Slave

Maude Pickett Smith

Edited by Lynn Veach Sadler

Maude Pickett Smith

Original title
Hester

Cover design
Sonja Smolec

Editors
Sonja Smolec
Yossi Faybish

Layout and Publishing
Aquillrelle

Cover image: Hester Pearsall, (approximately) 107, 1951, on the day she was interviewed by Maude Pickett Smith

ISBN 978-1-300-06371-1

Hester

Contents

Foreword

Hester is the story of an actual slave and is anchored in fact if recreated in imaginative detail. It is also an unusual and even remarkable example of race relations that, though begun in the awful days of slavery, worked on some level and continue to do so. After terrible experiences, Hester found sanctuary and a measure of peace with her last owners, the Parrotts, and she and their daughter, "Missy Mary," stayed in touch after the Civil War until Mary died.

This book is also very much the story of two amazing Duplin County, North Carolina, women—"Maude" (the author) and "Hester" (the subject of Maude's book), one White and one Black. Their lives were and *are* curiously and wonderfully intertwined, with Maude's family, especially her mother, a pivotal connection, as Maude is now.

Annie Maude Pickett (Smith), born 30 March 1928 and named for her grandmothers, is the daughter of Marjorie and Norman Pickett. Her brother Fred was born five years later. The family lived on a farm about three miles south of Magnolia (on the left side of Highway 117 in Duplin County). It was called "Buzzard Roost," though Maude never learned why. When the Picketts moved into town in 1937, she attended Magnolia School's eleven grades. She was at "ECTC" [East Carolina Teachers College in Greenville] 1945-46 and married Albert ("Abbie") Quinn Smith in 1946.

In the middle sixties, Maude was a substitute teacher and Secretary in the Principal's Office in Magnolia School. In charge of the school library, she worked with a young boy who had a learning disability for part of a school year and as a teacher's aide with first-graders at Rose Hill Christian School.

Leader of the local 4-H for seven years, Maude had among her members first-place earners in such areas as crafts, talent, and sewing and a national clothing winner. For three years, they sponsored a Heart Fund Drive and sent in, one year, more money per person than any other club in North Carolina.

7

Maude was a volunteer EMT on the Magnolia Rescue Squad for twenty years, had a hospice patient one year, and was named a Hospice Volunteer for the Year. In 1978, she was appointed by the Board of County Commissioners to the Citizen Advisory Committee for Community Development in Duplin County. While working with Magnolia's "Keep America Beautiful" program, she developed and presented a slide show. She was a board member for the Duplin County Hall of Fame and President of the Magnolia Historical Society.

Pianist/Organist sixty-three years and Sunday School teacher over fifty years at her church, Magnolia United Methodist, Maude has completed its history from the 1700's-2011 for publication. Also the Historian for Magnolia, she is compiling the town's history.

Like Hester, Maude has been of the greatest care-giving service to others. Her father-in-law lived with the family eight years, with Maude as his attendant; he died in her guest room at age ninety-seven. Her husband "Abbie" was sick many years, and, at the time of his death, 2000, her mother was living with them. She died, at age ninety-nine, in 2002, on a hospital bed at the foot of Maude's bed. Maude was her primary care-giver for six years.

Maude and her husband have two sons (Robert Nelson Smith and Albert Quinn Smith, Jr.),[1] five grandchildren, and twelve great-grandchildren. She continues to live in the family's home, two miles northeast of Magnolia, and owns, with her sons, Smith Brothers Gas Company and East Coast Water Conditioning Business.[2]

---

[1] A. Q., Jr., is actually the younger. Maude's grandfather and Abbie's grandmother were living when "Bobby" was born, so the Smiths chose to name the first son for the great grandparents. Maude says that, had they realized their second son was going to come so soon afterwards, they would have switched and had "A. Q., Jr.," first. The boys were eighteen months apart.

[2] Entrepreneurship is a hallmark of the family, whose works have included a golf course (developed in 1974 east of Magnolia) and a perpetual cemetery, Devotional Gardens, between Warsaw and Kenansville. See Maude Pickett Smith, "Three Generations Bring Service to Area of Duplin County," *The Heritage of Duplin County, North Carolina – 2012*. Wallace, NC: County Heritage, Inc. In press.

A lover of woodworking, Maude has made many pieces of furniture. She paints with oils and has had one-person art shows at Rose Hill's library and Kenansville's Fine Arts Building. History remains a hobby and joined her other great passion, writing, in the work on Hester Pearsall. In 2012, she purchased an historic home that was about to be destroyed.

Maude and Hester

By the time Maude trained in typing and shorthand at Miller Motte Business School in Wilmington (1952-53), she had already worked (1950-51) for *The Duplin Times* in Kenansville. She solicited advertising and did layouts for publishing ads, helped proofread, folded papers, wrote articles and feature stories about Duplin County, and traveled throughout it renewing subscriptions. Once a month, she wrote "Rambling in Duplin" about what she had seen and experienced during these travels.

The Duplin Times Editor, Robert ("Bob") Grady, had the idea for *The Duplin Story* as the culminating piece in the celebration of the County Bicentennial in 1949 and persuaded a friend, Broadway actor Sam Byrd, a writer in his own right, to create the outdoor drama. Bob must also have been responsible for having Hester Pearsall, the oldest-known living ex-slave in Duplin County, recognized during the second and final production of *The Duplin Story* (1950), though she did not want to stand up because she thought people would laugh at her for being so old.

Bob Grady, with Maude Smith, deserves major credit for working to preserve Black, as well as White, history and for advancing race relations. After the Centennial celebration was over, he assigned Maude to interview and write about Hester. In addition to *The Duplin Times*, the feature story was published in Goldsboro's *News Argus* and Wilmington's *Star News*.

What Bob did not know was that "Aunt Hester," as the Picketts fondly called her, midwifed when Maude was born. They lived in a small white cottage across the creek from Hester's family. Richard, Aunt Hester's son, sharecropped with Maude's father.

Maude knew his wife Josephine ("Ma Jo") and three of their children (Bernice, Carinese, and Hermenia). Junious had moved away, and she never knew Charles. Bernice, the oldest, swung her in her bassinet hanging from the living room ceiling, sang to her, and called her his "little princess." She and Hermenia were buddies. They "skinned the cat" in the Chinaberry tree, picked wild huckleberries, raided the watermelon patch, summoned doodlebugs, cooked and ate at the tobacco barn when Richard and Bernice were curing tobacco, and snared sparrows to roast in front of the fireplace. Maude rode the wagon to town with this family and attended functions at the children's school.

In May, 1951, when Maude set off for the interview, she was twenty-three. Hester, then a hundred and seven, lived with her daughter Mary Bethea and was sitting on the back porch when Maude arrived. Her black coat was pulled snuggly around her frail body, and a white cloth was wrapped around her head to keep the chill away. Her feet were extended onto the steps. When Maude told her who she was, Hester responded, "Oh, I does remember you. I was with your ma when you was born. You was a tiny little thing."

A few days before the interview, Hester had fallen down the back steps, was very sore, and ambulated with difficulty. Her income, fifteen dollars a month, was not sufficient to pay for her medicine. Nonetheless, she eventually led Maude into her bedroom, sat on the side of her bed, and opened a trunk to show her the dress and quilt she was sewing by hand. She could thread a needle and did not wear glasses, but her eyes appeared to Maude to be covered with a grey film.

Maude sat on the porch floor next to her and, after a bit of chatting, asked her to talk about her past. Looking into the distance, Hester began re-living her time as a slave. Maude quickly knew that what she was hearing would become a book about the ingenuity, stamina, and determination required to live the kind of life thrust upon that frail-yet-robust figure. In those days, underfed slaves cooked their meager rations in the fireplace. Men were issued two shirts, two pairs of pants, and one pair of shoes a year; women, two dresses and one pair of shoes. Children wore "shirts" until they were almost grown. If they outgrew their shoes or wore them out, they might have to go barefoot even in winter.

Hester sketchily traced her life from age four, when her mother Carol died, until the War Between the States ended (1865). Hester was around twenty, as close as Maude could come to estimating her age, given the unreliability of the slave census. Her mother belonged to "Mr. Bishop." Her father Sainty lived on another plantation, and she never knew his last name. She had a brother, William, but did not see him or her father again after she was sold on the auction block in Kenansville to "Mr. Miller." Some five years later, he sold her, also in Kenansville, to Mr. John A. Parrott, who lived near Kinston. After being freed, she asked to stay with the Parrotts. In effect, slavery left her without a family, money, or a place to go. Her grandmother finally found her and took Hester to her home in Magnolia. From these few facts came Maude's feature article and, ultimately, the careful and yet creative *Hester*. Maude was never able to find anyone in the family who knew the name of Hester's grandmother.

After moving to Magnolia, Hester met and married Essex Pearsall, who was twenty-seven years older. Their children were James, Henry, Richard, Mary, Louise, Lizzie, and Rosa. That little town once housed the world's largest bulb industry; and Hester, for the first time in her life, earned an income by cleaning and grading flower bulbs. She later became a midwife and helped Dr. Wessel, in Wilmington, deliver over five hundred babies as well as assisting approximately a hundred other doctors in birthing. While there, she lived with William and Eugenia Farmer and took care of their children. Their granddaughter, Alice Farmer Davis of Wilson, remembers Hester going to all their weddings and being there when babies were born.

Hester Pearsall developed pneumonia and died 23 September 1953. Her funeral service was held at Magnolia Baptist Church, where she was a member eighty-four years. She had told Maude: "Mr. Jack Nichols of Wilmington promised to buy my tombstone if I would care for his child. A while back I was sick. Mr. Nichols thought I was going to die. He brought the tombstone. I reckons I fooled him. The tombstone is in the loft of the barn out back." She was buried in the Magnolia Cemetery, and the stone was placed at her gravesite, but her granddaughter and Maude walked the cemetery, which has been vandalized and not maintained, and never found her grave. The granddaughter says that her father, Hester's son, and Hester were buried in the same plot and that a wagon wheel was placed at his grave. The granddaughter's mother was buried elsewhere because her husband's gravesite could not be found.

Hester's son Richard and his family lived on the farm where the Picketts resided until Maude was nine. They had a close relationship, and Maude's mother was very kind to the children, who loved her. In August, 1996, Hermenia and her family, descendants of Hester Pearsall and of Richard and Josephine Murphy Pearsall, honored Marjorie Pickett as their second mother. At the tribute, held at the Masonic Lodge in Wallace, Hermenia's nine children entertained with songs, read scripture, and gave Maude's mother gifts, including a dozen red roses. The emcee, Raymond Brown, grandson of Hermenia and great-grandson of Hester, said, "This is something we wanted to do while Mrs. Pickett is here to enjoy it. We wanted her to know how much we love her and her family." Maude has a video of the event "and enjoy[s] looking at it when [she] get[s] in the dumps."

Maude's desire to write, fueled in no small way by her involvement with Hester, became more and more urgent. In September 1999, she completed a beginning writer's course at the Institute of Children's Literature in West Redding, Connecticut, and, in August 2009, its advanced writing curriculum. Her Hester project led her to attend the North Carolina/South Carolina Writer's Conference in Durham (2007, 2009) and writing workshops at the Aqueduct (Chapel Hill) with Barbara Seuling and Esther Hershenham (a writing teacher at Ohio University). She is a member of the Society of Children's Book Writers and Illustrators.

Hester's descendants honor Marjorie Burton Pickett, mother of the author, Maude Pickett Smith, in August, 1996.

The Master of Ceremonies for the "Tribute to Marjorie Burton Pickett" was Raymond ("Petie") Brown, great-great-grandson of Hester and grandson of Hermenia Pearsall Stokes. He died in 2011.

13

Annie Maude Pickett Smith, daughter of Marjorie Burton Pickett and writer of *Hester*

Marjorie Burton Pickett

Left: Hermenia Pearsall Stokes
Right: Carinese ("Katie") Pearsall Shaw
Forefront: Marjorie Burton Pickett

14

Left to Right: Fred Pickett, brother of Maude Pickett Smith; Hermenia Pearsall Stokes, Hester's granddaughter and Maude's "pal" at the Pickett Farm; in the background, Hermenia's children; Maude; Marjorie Burton Pickett (foreground)

SHE TURNS 92—Marjorie Pickett of Magnolia, left, retired veteran of the Magnolia Rescue Squad, laughs with former squad member Carrie Lillie Gillespie at Mrs. Pickett's birthday reception.

Right: Carrie Lillie Pearsall Gillespie, who attended Mrs. Pickett's ninety-second birthday celebration (picture on the previous page), was Hester's granddaughter. Her father, Henry Pearsall (17 October 1912-25 November 2003), was Hester's son. Mrs. Pickett and Carrie were very close. According to Maude, Carrie was "like family." She walked to Mrs. Pickett's house almost every day to check on her, run errands, and help around the house.

Left to Right: Hermenia Pearsall Stokes; her husband, Deacon Jimmy Stokes; and Carinese ("Katie") Pearsall Shaw. The father of these granddaughters of Hester is Richard Pearsall.

16

Carrie Lillie Pearsall Gillespie,
Hester's granddaughter

Friends: Hermenia Pearsall
Stokes (Hester's granddaughter)
and Maude Pickett Smith

Tony Robinson, great-grandson of
Hester Pearsall; grandson of
Hester's daughter, Rosa Pearsall
Robinson, and Sivie Robinson;
son of Andrew Robinson, of Mt.
Olive, North Carolina, and Geralene
(Daniel) Robinson, of Whitakers,
North Carolina

Gwendolyn Bethea Vann, current
Mayor of Magnolia, North Carolina,
and great-granddaughter of Mary
Pearsall Bethea, Hester's daughter,
who was likely named for "Missy
Mary" Parrott

Parents of Maude Pickett Smith: Marjorie Burton Pickett and Norman Pickett

Annie Maude Pickett [Smith], Author-to-Be

Fiftieth Anniversary of Albert Quinn ("Abbie") Smith, Sr., and Maude Pickett Smith, middle couple. Couple on the left: daughter-in-law Patsy and son Bobby. Couple on the right: daughter-in-law Sharon and son A. Q., Jr.

My Involvement

Although I grew up in Duplin County, I was graduated from high school in Lee County and happen to have returned there to live. I met Maude when I became the Editor of *Footnotes*, the journal published by The Duplin County Historical Society, and am especially indebted to her for such contributions as an article on Macy Cox, an outstanding Magnolia citizen. She shared *Ecclesia's* memorial number (1933) about Margaret Kelly, who, with her husband, George M. Kelly, both Magnolia residents, became missionaries in China (September 1910). She also lent the complete script, with annotations, of *The Duplin Story*, as preserved by

19

Margaret Gurley Fussell and with her accompanying scrapbook and amazing memorabilia, now published in book form.[3]

In January, 2012, Tony Robinson, Hester's great-grandson, the grandson of her daughter Rosa, visited Maude for some three hours. She read some of the book manuscript to him and gave him pictures of Hester and a copy of the article in *Footnotes*.[4] They drove by the house where Maude interviewed Hester and went to the Magnolia Cemetery. Tony returned in March but still could not find Hester's grave.

I also write a column, "Sadler (But Wiser)," for the on-line newspaper, *Lee County Star-Tribune*. Of course, it has to have a Lee County connection. I never imagined having one unexpectedly presented to me via my Duplin project on Maude's Hester. Then I discovered that *Tony Robinson lives in Sanford* (as I do)![5]

(Dr.) Lynn Veach Sadler
Sanford, North Carolina
May 2012

---

[3] *The Duplin Story: An Historical Play With Music By Sam Byrd*. Ed. Lynn Veach Sadler. Kenansville, NC: Press of The Duplin County Historical Society, 2011.

[4] Lynn Veach Sadler, "'Maude' and 'Hester': Duplin Women," *Footnotes*, 116 (2011): 2-4.

[5] See Lynn Veach Sadler, Column No. 69, "In Praise of Coincidence," *Lee County Star-Tribune*—http://lee.countync.us/columnists. [I also have a relationship comparable to that of Hester and her family and the Smiths: one of my former undergraduate students, Ret. Lieutenant Colonel Karen Dixon-Brugh, who recently received her Ph.D., considers me her "godmother"; she is African-American, and I am White.]

Acknowledgments

I thank

—Barbara Seuling for encouraging me when I was ready to quit. I would never have written this story if she hadn't told me she liked it and said, "Write it, Maude!"

—(Dr.) Lynn Veach Sadler for editing my book and helping me get it published as well as for all the help she has unselfishly given and, especially, for being my friend.

—Liza Swazey and Kevin McColley, instructors of the Institute of Children's Literature, for getting me started writing.

—Celestine Davis for telling me to "write so a blind person can see," encouraging me to get published, and helping me in many, many ways to make my story better.

—Elizabeth Pope for encouragement and for help with the research.

—Stephen Stoikes for critiquing my work and offering suggestions.

—Barri Piner for encouragement and critiques.

—Jacqueline Hall for listening to my story over and over and over and for encouraging me to keep going.

—Jeffrey J. Crow, Paul D. Escott, and Flora J. Hatley for use of their *A History of African Americans in North Carolina* (Raleigh: Division of Archives and History, North Carolina Department of Cultural Resources, 1992).

—My sons and their wives (Bobby; Patsy; A. Q., Jr.; and Sharon) for being excited about my story, encouraging me, and saying, "Get it published, Mom!"

Maude Pickett Smith
August, 2012

Hester

Chapter 1

Hester Heartbroken

Outside the cabin, four-year-old Hester squirmed, twisted, then slid from the stump, scraping and scratching her bare bottom. Her feet felt hot as they touched the sandy yard. The overhead sun was slipping behind the pine trees at the end of the cotton field. Her shirt, tattered from many washings with lye soap, was the only garment she wore. It did little to keep her back from scorching. She ran to the shady side of the cabin, wiggled her toes into the cooler sand. The shade felt good. Her tears were suddenly a brackish river tracing her ashy, ebony cheeks and making salty deposits in her mouth.

"Why won't Ma and Bessie let me in de cabin?" She already knew life was full of uncertainty, but the crying going on inside frightened her. She ran to the door. "Ma, dat you cryin'? Ma, why you won't let me in?" Panic. Finally, Bessie stood framed in the doorway, looking taller than usual. Hester stared at the sweat dripping off her thin, boney nose and running down her honey-colored face. Something was wrong.

Brushing tears away, Hester followed Bessie into her dreary, smoke-filled cabin, even darker after the bright sunlight. It wasn't smoke from good stuff cooking in the fireplace, but Bessie had heated water in the iron kettle. She could tell that much.

When her eyes adjusted to the darkness, Hester saw her mother lying on Bessie's cot, went to her as fast as her small feet would take her. Sweat stood out on the tired-looking face. The thin gown looked all wet and stuck to her body. "Ma, why you on Bessie's bed? You don't sleep on no cot. You sleeps on a straw mattress on the dirt floor wit me. What be wrong wit you, Ma? Is you sick?"

"Everthing fine, Hester Girl. Jist look what I has."

Hester saw that Ma was holding a baby. It started screaming as she stood there and stared. "Ma, make dat baby stop cryin'. It hurtin'?"

"No, Hester. When babies born, dey cries. Cryin' make dere lungs strong."

"Who baby be dat, Ma?"

"*My* baby, Hester. He William, yo baby brother."

Hester reached out and touched the baby's soft hand. Little William took a firm grip on her finger. Excited, she touched her face with that tiny hand.

Carol Bishop and her daughter Hester were slaves on the Tom Bishop Plantation near Kinston, in Lenoir County, North Carolina, where Hester was born in 1844. They shared the crude, one-room log cabin with Bessie, her husband, and their four children.

A few weeks before William was born, Hester had asked her mother: "Why ain't I got no Pa livin' wit me like Bessie's chillens?"

"Hester, your Pa belong to 'nother massa, live at 'nother plantation. He has to use his mastah last name, be wit him. He can't live wit us. His name Sainty. He love you very much."

Two days after Carol gave birth, Hester watched her mother walk gingerly outside the cabin to wash the clothes for the Bishops as well as Bessie's family and her own. She had no choice, but lifting the heavy wet clothes was difficult. Hester followed her to the box where she placed little William so she could keep an eye on him as she washed the clothes. The leaves on the oak tree moved in the breeze. Wooden tubs sat on a bench beside the cabin. Hester's mother wasn't strong enough to get water from the creek to fill them and the wash pot, so Freeman, a young slave boy, stayed home from the field to fetch it for her.

"Ma, little William sleepin'. I ain't got nothin' to do. Can I go to de crick wit Freeman? Can I, Ma?"

"I spose so, Hester, but you stay wit him!"

Hester ran along behind Freeman. Tall pines, sweet gums, and oaks lined the way. Skipping over to the wild honeysuckle, she broke off a blossom and smelled the sweetness. The morning glories with their pretty blue- and rose-colored blossoms weaving throughout the weeds fascinated her. She felt free as a bird, had no worries.

At the creek, Freeman rolled up his dirty pants legs and walked into the clear, cool water. He dipped one bucket full, then the other. Hester paddled around in the water and splashed some on him. Freeman didn't seem to mind. She knew the cool water felt good to his hot, sweaty body.

"Hester, come on, we's got to get back to the cabin. I's got to get mo warter to fill yo ma's tubs and wash pot."

Hester followed Freeman, stepping in the little puddles the water made as it sloshed from the buckets.

At the cabin, a large iron pot with three legs was raised up on bricks. Under it, Freeman placed pieces of fat lightwood strips chipped from stumps left in the woods a long time. Hester liked to watch the sticky resin ooze out. It made the fire burn quickly. Freeman placed pieces of oak on top of the lightwood.

"Ma, I waded in the warter at the creek. Felt cool. Dem pretty flowers beside de road smelt good. It fun."

"Did you mind Freeman, Hester?"

"Yassum, stayed right wit him, Ma."

Hester crawled onto the bench beside the tubs, dipped her fingers in the cool water as her mother punched the dirty clothes with her hands, using lye soap to wash them. She struggled to lift the heavy wet clothes into another tub and rinse off the soap. Knowing she was not allowed near the wash pot of boiling water, Hester slipped from the bench and skipped over to William. Carol, using a wooden paddle, took the heavy wet clothes over to the black, iron pot and put them into the boiling water, careful her long skirt didn't catch fire.

Sitting on the ground by the baby, Hester patted him on a little hand, looked him in the eye, and said, "Little William, I's glad I gots a brother. I loves you. Us gonna have a good time when you gets bigger. Gonna be fam'ly."

Suddenly, her mother screamed. Hester ran to her. "Ma!

Ma! What de matter? Does you hurt?"

"Hester, run to de corn field by de barn. Tell Bessie I sick, needs her. Got pain burnin' bad in ma back, ma stomach." Carol was bent over.

Hester ran as fast as her legs would pump. "Bessie, Bessie, come quick! Ma hurtin'. Her be sick, needin' help."

Not knowing what was happening, the overseer let Bessie leave the field. One look told her. "Hester, you goes to de Great House, tell Marse Bishop to fetch de docter causin' yo ma bad took."

Hester ran as though hot sand was blistering her bare feet. She was screaming for Marse Bishop. Running up on the porch, she banged on the door. Looking very disgusted, he opened the screen door and stepped out to see what the problem was with the frantic child.

"Marse Bishop, please fetch de doctor. My ma sick. Her's hurtin', needin' help. Her's got me and a baby boy to look after. I don't want nothin' happenin' to my ma. Please hurry, Marse Bishop!"

The man looked down at her. "You go on back to where you belong. Your ma will be alright."

Hester thought, "You one mean man."

"Bessie, Marse Bishop ain't sendin' for no docter. He say

Ma be alright."

Pacing the floor and wringing her hands, Bessie mumbled, "I knowed Carol oughten lift dem heavy clothes atter birthin' dat baby. She bleedin'. I ain't knowin' how to stop it."

Hester prayed, "Lord, please make Ma well." She pulled her pallet up close to Bessie's cot where Carol stayed all that night. "Bessie, is my ma goin' to be alright?"

"Hester, I'm gonna take care of your ma. You goes to sleep."

Hester remained quiet but didn't sleep. She watched Bessie put cool cloths on her mother's forehead, but they didn't bring down the fever. In the wee hours, she died. Hester saw tears running down Bessie's face. She had never seen Bessie cry before. "Bessie, why you cryin'?"

Drying tears, Bessie soothed. "Hester, everything gonna be alright. I jist tired."

The cabin was silent. Evening was approaching, casting shadows through the open door. A neighbor took Little William home to her cabin.

Hester was angry. "Why dey take my baby brother away?" She couldn't understand what was happening.

Hester's ma didn't look at her with her sad eyes as before. "Ma, why ain't you talkin' to me?" Maybe she was just resting.

Standing beside the cot, Hester reached out and touched her arm, but Carol didn't move. She always smiled and talked to Hester, but now she didn't even look at her. Hester remembered being on her lap, being held close and told, "Hester, I loves you and will always keep you safe." So why was her mother not talking to her now? Hester was afraid. Since Ma had a baby boy, maybe she didn't love her any more.

Bessie put her finger on Carol's eyes, gently closed them, and pulled a cloth over her face. "Bessie, why you closin' Ma's eyes an' puttin' dat cloth on her face? Is you helpin' her sleep?" Bessie didn't answer. Hester thought maybe she did it to keep the flies from bothering Ma while she slept.

Arriving home from the fields, the slaves stood in Bessie's yard with their heads bowed. One of them said, "Ifen Marse Bishop been a carin' owner, send fo a docter, maybe Carol live." They were sad and shook their heads in anger as they walked to their cabins.

There was no way of preserving the body. Carol must be buried soon.

Bessie walked slowly, thinking over all that had happened the last few hours. Sad and angry, she dreaded facing Marse Bishop. Arriving at the Great House, she sent a slave to ask him to come outside so she could speak to him. The longer she waited, the angrier she became. When he finally came out, Bessie stared him straight in the eyes and said, "Marse Bishop, Carol die. Ifen you had get a doctur, she maybe live. We is got to have a funeral soon. I wants permission to bury her at de cemetery up on de hill. I wants permission fo her friends to get offen work so dey can go to dat funeral."

"Bessie, you have permission to bury her on the hill, and I will let a few hands off for two hours, so you had better have a quick service."

Back at the cabin, Bessie took little Hester onto her lap, and, looking into her sad eyes, said, "Hester, you knows yo ma sick. Child, she die, won't be wit us no more."

"What you mean won't be wit us no more? Her can't leave me. Her my ma. I needs Ma here wit me. Her can't go nowhere witouten me." Hester began sobbing. She didn't understand what was happening. She didn't understand dying. She was heartbroken.

Hester

Chapter 2
Ma Gone

"Ma, you git up off Bessie cot! Why don't you talk to me no more? Why Little William be took away? He our baby. Need to be here wit us, not to Carrie's."

"Bessie, why dem womens in yo house? Dey sposed to be in de field workin'." Hester was afraid. The women's faces were hard with sadness and a sense of duty. No longer laughing and chattering as usual, they skillfully worked together as they dressed Hester's mother in her best, a thin cotton dress mud-colored from the lye soap. She'd stitched the hem by candlelight. Hester went to a dark corner in the cabin and sat on some rags. She didn't want to be around the women. They acted funny. Something strange was happening. "Bessie, why can't Ma put her dress on by herself when she wake up?"

"I'll tell you later, Hester" was all Bessie replied. But she thought to herself, "Somebody got to go over to dat next plantation, tell Sainty de news."

A slave leaving the plantation without permission from the owner was punished severely, but Richard was Sainty's friend. "Bessie, I go tell Sainty."

"Thanks to you, Richard. Tell him de buryin' be in de mornin'."

Richard waited until dark, slipped into the woods. He crept in the darkness as quietly as possible. When a screech owl screeched over his head, he fell to the ground, thinking it might be a bounty hunter after a runaway slave. Finally, he got slowly to his feet and continued his journey. After reaching the other plantation and staying in the dark shadows, he quietly crept up to each cabin and called out, as softly as possible, "Sainty, you dere?"

Finally Sainty asked, "Richard, dat be you?"

The two men stepped away from the cabin into the darkness. "Sainty, I's got good news fo you but mo bad news."

"Richard, tell me de good news fust."

"Well, Sainty, you has a baby boy."

"Oh my, dat fo sure good news. What de bad? Baby die?"

"No, Sainty. I hates to tell you. Yo wife Carol she die."

"Man, don't come here tellin' me dat. Can't be. Someday

we goin' to git to lives togither. When Carol be buried?"

"She be buried in de mornin' up at de cemetery on de hill our plantation. Believes yo mastah lets you come?"

"I be dere, Richard. One way or nuther. I be dere."

The dense forest with underbrush spreading upward and outward between the trees embraced the night. The path was visible only when moonlight pierced the darkness. Hoot owls screeched overhead. Wolves howled in the distance. They could have been an overseer on the prowl. Overseers used all types of signals. Richard walked quietly, listened to all noises. At daybreak, he arrived home.

Hester came from the cabin and saw Richard at the shed nailing boards together into some kind of box. "Richard, what you gone do wit dat?" She was so interested in what was going on she didn't realize he hadn't answered. She watched as Bessie put in soft rags. Two slaves picked Hester's mother up and gently laid her in the box. Why was Richard nailing a lid on the box with her mother in it? Hester watched curiously, then followed the slaves, saw them heave the box onto a wagon pulled by a mule.

Bessie took her hand. "Come wit me, Hester." The two of them walked behind the wagon. Following closely after them, the other slaves sang "Shall We Gather at the River" and "Amazing Grace." The beautiful songs echoed across the fields.

At the graveside, Richard said, "Whoa," as he pulled on the lines to stop the mule.

Hester walked around the wagon with Bessie and saw a hole with a pile of dirt beside it. The slaves placed the box on two ropes and slowly lowered it into the hole. "Oh, Ma!" Hester cried. She screamed at the men. "Don't put Ma in dat hole! Her got to go home wit me!"

A thump. Richard had thrown the first shovel of dirt on top of the box. Hester ran to look in. Pulling on Richard's pants leg, she screamed, "Richard, stop dat! You can't put dirt on Ma!" She sobbed.

Sainty took a few steps towards his daughter but stopped. She hadn't seen him for a good while. She'd be frightened if he touched her.

Bessie reached out, took Hester in her arms and held her closely, gently rubbing her back. "Shhh, child. Shhh, child."

Hester buried her face in Bessie's bosom and kept crying.

Reverend Robinson said a few words and prayed. The slaves huddled around the grave and softly hummed spirituals. At Bessie's direction, Hester placed a small bunch of wild yellow daisies on Carol's grave. Richard drove a handmade wooden cross into the soft dirt at its head.

Bessie cradled Hester close and walked back to the cabin humming softly in her ear. Hester's tears stopped, but she was snubbing. Bessie could feel her little body quivering as she held her close. Hester was heartbroken.

Hester relaxed and fell asleep as Bessie cradled her in her arms and sang, "Sleep Little Baby Sleep." Bessie laid the sleeping child onto the rags in the corner and ran her fingers across Hester's tear-streaked cheeks.

Sainty came into the cabin. "Bessie, kin I sees Hester one mo time afore I goes back to de plantation?"

"Of course you can, Sainty."

As he knelt beside the sleeping child, Bessie went next door and got little William. She thought Sainty should see his new son before going home.

Sainty leaned closer to Hester and looked into her face. He knew the child was heartbroken, wondered what was going to become of her. He wished he could take her with him but knew better.

Bessie brought little William and handed him to Sainty. He gently took the baby into his hands and looked into his face, studying each and every feature. Then he held him close to his heart and said, "Son, I wishes I could take you and Hester wit me. Maybe someday dat will happen." He turned to Bessie, handed her the baby, and thanked her for all she had done for his family. "Bessie, please take care of my children." He walked out the door and into the woods for his journey back to the plantation where he lived.

Chapter 3

Hester's First Job

Bessie kept Hester. She was small for her age and would continue to be so because she and her adopted family had very little to eat, and it was tasteless and the same each day. Mr. Bishop's main concern was that they get to work on time and work hard.[6] He gave them a small amount of fat pork and cornmeal and sometimes a bit of coffee and molasses. To add variety, Bessie occasionally made kush,[7] a spicy improvement on regular cornbread. Sitting on the rough-hewn benches at the crude table, the family ate fat pork and cornbread for breakfast. Bessie and her

---

[6]After working all day in the fields, slaves had other jobs before going to bed and ended so exhausted that they fell on their straw mattresses without bathing. Men fed and watered the livestock and repaired tools. Boys cut wood and stacked it by the fireplace and brought water from the creek in wooden buckets for drinking, bathing, and cooking. Women bathed the children, cooked the meals, made clothes . . . .

[7]Kush was cornmeal, onions, and red peppers mixed with water and cooked on the coals.

husband drank weak coffee, and the children had water.

When the sun peeped over the horizon, Hester, Bessie, and the other slaves were required to be in the field. Bessie bundled the baby under one arm and pulled the field crib with the other. It had a square bottom made of wooden boards. Four posts cut from small tree trunks were nailed to the corners. Netting was pulled around the frame and fastened to the posts. She put the crib down at the end of the cotton rows and thought they looked longer than usual. She dreaded the day's work.

Surrounding the amber-colored, hollowed-out gourd with both arms, Hester pressed it tight to her stomach as she trudged behind Bessie. She knew if she dropped it in the dirt, the bread and fat pork Bessie had put in that morning would be ruined, and they would have no lunch. The smell was so wonderful Hester felt she could eat every bite, but they had to wait until the sun was straight overhead.

"Hester, hurry up. Quit draggin' yo feet in dat dirt. You knows we'uns got to get to dat field." Bessie didn't realize how difficult it was for Hester to carry the large gourd.

Other slave children kept chickens out of Mr. Bishop's garden, toted water to the field for the workers, collected kindling for fires, or cleaned the yards. Because she was only five, Hester watched the baby. Standing on tiptoes, she reached over the side of the crib and shooed flies away with a small leafy branch.

The cotton rows were so long Hester couldn't always see the others, making her afraid until she heard their "Swing Low, Sweet Chariot." Singing seemed to make the day go by a little faster, but time still went like a terrapin. "I knows what I'll do. Lil' William gone to sleep. I'll make toad frog houses. She wiggled her toes in the dirt, packed it down on top of her foot, then pulled out her foot. The "house" had an opening so a little frog could go in and stay. Sometimes Hester stepped on the frog house and smashed it, then built another one. "I jist knows it be eatin' time. I is so hungry." Looking up, she found the sun straight over her head. The others were putting down their hoes and heading for her shade tree. Their threadbare, sweaty clothes stuck to their bodies as they plopped down on the ground under it. Reaching into their gourds, they began eating their bit of fat pork and cornbread. Hester used a gourd dipper to give each one a drink from the water bucket. They had thirty minutes to eat and rest.

Hester stood by while Bessie fed William. "Bessie, Lil' William go to sleep, and I make toad frog houses."

"I'll bet dat fun."

"Yassum. Sho was. You see how many I made?"

"You sho was busy, Hester."

"Well, I didn't have nothin' else to do."

At night when Hester crawled onto her pallet on the dirt floor, she'd wonder if she'd always be hungry and tired and wished she could stay in a pretty two-story house like the Bishops had. "Maybe someday I'll live somewhere like dat and lie down in dat cool green grass under a big shade tree." Tears streamed down Hester's face as she thought about the things she was missing out on. "Ma, I misses you so bad!"

Chapter 4

Hester in Trouble

"I's so tired. I thinks I stay in de cabin in de morning. I don't think de others miss me ifen I stays. But I knows better dan dat. I knows if I does, and Mr. Bishop find out, his mean old overseer whip me good. I knows he will causin' I saw im whip a girl one day. I thought fo sure her goin' to die, an her thirteen." Hiding behind the cabin, Hester had peeped out to see what was happening. The girl was screaming, crying, and begging. Raising his hand high above his head, the overseer hit her with strips of cowhide fastened to a stick. The whip wrapped around her body and made cuts in her flesh. Hester cringed at every lick the girl received. Blood ran down her body onto the ground. After the overseer left, Hester slipped out to the girl and washed her wounds with cool water. "I can't think 'bout dat no more. It too terrible. I ain't gonna stay in dat cabin in de mornin' either."

But the time came when she did. Waking up, Hester stretched her arms over her head, squinted her eyes, looked around the cabin, and knew something was wrong. No sunlight was coming in, and she thought it was still dark outside. She didn't hear anything, believed everybody was asleep. Had she waked up too early? Then she realized there was no snoring or any signs of anyone being there. Rubbing her eyes with her fists, trying to see better, she realized no one was in the cabin but her. How had she not smelled food cooking? Her heart leapt. She was late! Jumping from her straw mattress, she pulled her shirt over her head and ran out the door for the field.

"Lord have mercy, I knows dey's gonna miss me when dey puts de baby in de field crib. If somebody sees I late, I be in big trouble." Maybe no one saw her. Maybe she would be lucky this time.

But someone did see her and told the overseer. He reported her to Mr. Bishop, who sent for her to come to the Great House. Hester tried to take as long as possible to get there. Who told him about her being late? Why would anyone do that?

With her head bowed, Hester slowly walked up the steps and stood in front of Mr. Bishop, who was standing on the back porch waiting for her. She was very frightened of getting a whipping.

Mr. Bishop was tall and skinny and had a nose as big and lumpy as a potato. From the moment he looked down at the scrawny slip of a child craning her neck to see the length of him, he made up his mind to sell Hester. His dark, mean eyes sent a shiver up her spine.

"Girl, why were you late going to the field this morning? Don't you know you are supposed to be there at sun-up?"

"Yassuh, Marse Bishop, I's sorry. I was jist so tired. I didn't wake up. De rest in a hurry and forget to call me. I won't do it no more, Marse Bishop. I promises. Please don't whip me," she pleaded.

"Girl, you go back to the hut and get your things together. In the morning, you and I are going to the Auction Market. I'm going to sell you."

Hester could not imagine what an Auction Market was but knew it had to be something terrible. On the way back to the cabin, she had many things running through her mind. "What gonna happen to me? I wishes he whip me. If he sell me, I never sees Carrie or Bessie or William agin. I won't be able to go to Ma's grave and put flowers on it, an I'll never see Pa agin.

Oh lordy, I jist wants to die. I sho does miss you, Ma," she said outloud.

Bessie saw the small girl stumbling along the path carrying the weight of the world on her shoulders and expected the worst.

"Bessie, Mr. Bishop say he gonna sell me. I's got to see William 'fore I goes."

As Hester walked in the door at the cabin next door where Little William lived, he reached out his arms to her. His little face lit up, and his teeth sparkled white as snow. Sitting on the dirt floor, Hester pulled him onto her lap and squeezed him, never wanting to let go. Looking into his brown, twinkling eyes, she said, "Little William, I's gonna be gone from here, and I sho hopes you won't forgets me. I loves you, William." She tried to hide the tears from her brother, but one of his little pudgy hands reached up and wiped one away.

"Hester, when William get older, I tells him about you," Bessie said.

It was a sad time the next morning when Mr. Bishop drove his horse and buggy up to Bessie's door.

"Bessie, get that girl out here right now."

"Yassuh," Bessie responded.

Bessie called out to Hester. She was nowhere to be found

and didn't answer. "Hester, you come out now! If you don't, Mr. Bishop will beat the hide off both us."

Hester crawled from under a pile of rags. She didn't want to get whipped, but she didn't want Bessie hurt either.

Picking her up and holding her close, Bessie said, "Hester, always remember I loves you. Maybe someday we be togither agin."

Hester clung to Bessie as she tried to put the sobbing girl in the back of the buggy.

"Quit that crying and straighten up, girl. I mean *right now!*" Mr. Bishop scolded.

Hester sat in the back of the buggy and waved to Bessie as long as she could see her.[8] "I wonders what Bessie and dem others doin' right now. Probly choppin' cotton. I wonder who lookin' after de baby. I knows he gonna miss me. I knows I misses him already." Hester was petrified. She had never been away from the plantation. She had heard the Auction Market was where slaves were sold away from their families. Why couldn't she have a family? Her ma was gone, and now she would miss seeing William and Bessie and everybody. She wouldn't be able to put flowers on her mother's grave. There

---

[8]Hester later learned that Mr. Bishop took her to the slave market in Kenansville, North Carolina, about forty miles from Kinston.

would be no one to keep her safe. Would she ever see her family again? What was going to happen to her? She had never felt more alone.

Chapter 5
The Slave Market

Deep ruts cut into the sandy road. Hester felt uneasy. Her knees, bottom, and elbows hurt from bouncing around on the floor of the buckboard. Holding on tightly, she wondered how far they still had to go. She really needed to make a trip into the woods but was afraid to tell Mr. Bishop. She was also thirsty, could almost taste the cool water from the creek back home. Dust sent flying by the wheels turning in the sand made the air stifling. Mr. Bishop tapped the horse on his rump with his whip, and he spurted on. Hester clutched the side of the buggy to keep from falling off. "I wishes I workin' in de cotton field back home," she thought. "At least I know what hapnen'."

When they arrived, Hester saw slaves chained together like cattle. Their masters rode horses behind them. If they didn't walk fast enough, they were lashed with cowhide whips. They looked hot and tired. Hester figured they were thirsty. She knew she was.

Large elm trees lined the road circling the courthouse near the Auction Market in Kenansville. The horses at the hitching posts switched their tails to shoo away the biting flies. Mr. Bishop's snorted and flopped his head from side to side, shaking drippings from his nose. He had been run hard for the forty or so miles to Kenansville. A lot of people were milling around.

Mr. Bishop lifted Hester from the buggy and put her on the ground. Everything was so new to her. She couldn't take it all in. Suddenly she realized that Mr. Bishop had walked away from her, and she ran to catch up. He went down the small log steps to a pipe with water running from it. She would learn that this was a natural spring[9] used for many years. He cupped his hands together and drank the cool water from them. After he finished, Hester did the same. Even though the water tasted good, she didn't tarry long. She didn't want to get lost from Mr. Bishop because she had never been to town or anywhere else away from the plantation. Even though she was uneasy about what was going to happen to her, she knew she couldn't run

---

[9]Henry Gaster, born in Holland (1726), came through Duplin County and, with his widowed sister Barbara, who reportedly discovered the spring in Kenansville, moved on to live in present Lee County.

away and hide. She didn't know how to or where to go.

Menfolk stood around. Having no women, not even slave women there, made her nervous. Most times, she remembered Bessie telling her, White women didn't go to places like this. Their husbands decided what slaves to buy.

At the courthouse was a large platform, like a floor built up on posts, just high enough so the men could study the slaves. Hester didn't realize it was where she would be sold or what being sold meant. A few pretty houses and some stores were built along the road, but she didn't know what they were. She really wasn't too interested. She was more concerned about what was going to happen to her.

The slaves she'd seen on the way into town were standing naked on the platform. Naked except for their "shackles." Masters stood by watching. She'd heard Bessie and some of the others back home talking. Slaves were stripped naked so the buyers could see if they had been whipped for doing something wrong. If they had scars and welts, they were not good slaves and didn't bring much money. Usually slaves were sold in December so the owner could use them or hire them out come January. They had to take their clothes off even if it was bad cold. It didn't matter to the masters how cold they were. To them, they were no more important than animals.

It was summer now, so these slaves were being sold, including her, because their owners wanted to get rid of them. They were nothing but trouble. "Oh lordy me, I sho hopes I don't have to take my shirt off." Hester was quivering, scared. "What in dis world gonna happen to me?"

A big White man led Hester up the steps onto the auction block. He told her in his deep voice, "I don't know why anyone would want a little mite like you." He left Hester standing on the large platform by herself. She was just happy she didn't have to take her shirt off.

But what happened was worse. She was unable to hold back any longer. She wet herself. It was running down her legs into the worn-out shoes she'd been allowed to have for the trip. Her toes felt cramped, as though they were breaking, and now they were getting wet. The men laughed at her. She wanted to run and hide. All eyes were on her.

"I wonders what man goin' to buy me? I sho hopes he be good an kind."

One of those standing out front was short and fat with hair graying at the temples. An unlighted pipe looked as though it would fall from his mouth, but what she noticed most was the frown on his face. She thought he must be mad with the world. She hoped he wouldn't buy her. He wouldn't be a good master.

The man who'd led her up to the platform was talking faster and faster, and then she heard him say, "Going once, going twice, going three times. Sold to Mr. Miller!"

"Who be Mr. Miller?" Hester wondered. Whoever he was, he could see she was small, Hester reckoned. She wouldn't take up much room and wouldn't eat much, but he would make her work hard. He didn't have to pay much for her. Then she saw the short fat man with the pipe in his mouth. He was the man who looked so unhappy. He was coming for her. "Oh no, not *dat* man!"

She learned soon enough that Mr. Miller was no better than Mr. Bishop. He plopped her on the buckboard behind the seat like a bag of salt. Lashing the flanks of the horse with the lines, he shouted, "Git up there!" The sudden jerk of the cart nearly threw Hester out on her head.

The wheels sent sand into Hester's eyes, nose, and mouth. Tears washed some of the dirt from her eyes. Hester wanted to see where she was going, but she was riding backwards and couldn't.

When they arrived at the Great House of her new life, Hester peeped around the side of the buckboard. She saw fat Mrs. Miller standing at the gate. Her dark dress bulged at the seams, and the bonnet fitted tight to her face and tied under her chin. Hester had never seen anyone so fat and ugly. She looked as though she was choking. Disgusted when she saw that Hester had wet herself, Mrs. Miller yelled at Josephine, a slave girl standing near-by, "Get this girl cleaned up. Get her out of my sight!"

Hester thought, "I jist knows her ain't gonna be kind and good. Her don't care nothin' 'bout us slaves."

The big red sun was going down behind the trees, and darkness was slipping in. When they arrived at Josephine's cabin, five children were standing at the door wondering where their mother had found that girl. With all those children, Hester was worried. "Will there be enough room for me?"

The one-room cabin, much like Bessie's, had a rough table, homemade benches, and a fireplace with a makeshift pie safe on another wall. Josephine didn't know what she was going to do with Hester. The cabin was too small to hold another person. And who would look after this girl? "I will find a little space in a corner somewhere," Josephine thought. She poured warm water from the iron kettle sitting in the coals of the fireplace into a large wooden tub.

Hester took her dirty shirt off, dropped it on the floor, and put one foot in the tub, then the other. "Dis here warm warter feel good."

Josephine used lye soap to bathe Hester, then put a clean shirt on her and asked if she wanted something to eat.

"Yasam, I is a little hongry."

"I has a little I kin gives you."

"Dat alright," Hester replied. Sitting on the bench at the table, she pinched off small pieces of the bread and ate a few bites of fatback. The food tasted good, but she was so tired. Josephine led her to a corner and spread some rags on the dirt floor. Hester lay down on them and was soon asleep.

Josephine wondered who Hester's ma was and where she had come from. She was so small and young to be sent away from her family. Why did Hester have to leave the other plantation? She sat at the table and prayed she could help Hester love her new family.

Hester

Chapter 6

Hester Sold Again

Hester, now ten, was devastated. After living with Josephine and her family on the Miller Plantation for five years and learning to love them, she was to be sold again. "What I gone do? Is I ever havin' a home and family? Evertime I feels I's got one and loves dem, Massa sell me." Thoughts of being on the auction block in front of all the White men made her sick to her stomach. What if she wet herself again? Most of her life, she had been sad and shed tears. Would she ever find happiness?

Hester had learned a valuable lesson at the Miller Plantation she would never forget. A man slave was plowing the cornfield. He was a quiet, good worker who gave no trouble, and the overseer didn't pay much attention to him. At the end of the corn row was a woods with tall pines, oaks, and thick underbrush. For a long while, he had been thinking and planning how to run away. The time came. He turned the mule with the plow around, heading him back to the plantation. Then he walked into the woods as if to relieve himself. As soon as he was out of sight, he started running as fast as he could. The briars tore at his clothes and face, and he fell over rotten logs, but he scrambled up and kept going. He had to get as far away as possible before dark.

The mule knew it was feeding time and headed for the plantation with the plow bumping along behind. When he arrived, the overseer instantly knew the slave had run away.

Hester wondered what was happening. She heard Mr. Miller and the other men yelling to one another as they straddled their horses. The foxhound dogs were turned loose. They barked ferociously and headed for the woods. The deep brush didn't stop them, and the men on horseback were close behind. They came to the creek and lost the man's scent but picked it up again on the other side. Soon they found the exhausted slave huddled next to a tree with his head in his hands. He knew what was coming. Mr. Miller and the men tied a rope around his body, threw him over a horse, and headed back home. At the plantation, they went to the slave quarters. Removing the rope from the slave, they tied his hands together and threw the rope over a tree limb. He was pulled up until his feet didn't touch the ground. They took turns giving him lashes with a whip.

The slaves didn't leave their cabins, but Mr. Miller knew they were watching. The rope was let loose, and the unconscious man fell to the ground. After the beaters left, the man's wife and friends came out, picked him up, and carried him into the cabin where his wife tended his wounds and comforted him. Hester made up her mind she would never, never try to run away.

All Hester had to take with her when she left the Miller Plantation was a pair of handed-down, worn-out shoes, too small for her, and two wash-faded shirts.

Mr. Miller lifted Hester from the back of the buckboard and put her down on the hot sand. They had arrived at the Auction Market in Kenansville. It didn't seem as far to Hester as it had five years before. "I wonders if Massa Miller gonna drink warter from dat spring like Massa Bishop." Sure enough, he went to the overflow, cupped his hands to let the water pool into them, and drank. After he walked away, Hester drank. It felt good to her bare feet as she stood in the water flowing from the pipe and puddling on the ground.

She was on the auction block again. Gazing into the faces of the men out front, she looked for someone she thought would like her and take care of her. She knew more what to expect this time. A tall, handsome man was smiling and speaking to everyone. He wore a large straw hat, store-bought clothes, and shiny black boots. His hair and twinkling eyes were dark brown. "I jist knows he de one will buy me. I sho hopes so." The high hopes made her less nervous. She began looking around. From the auction block, she saw people going in and out of the courthouse, wondered what was going on there.

Smelling food cooking at the hotel made her realize how hungry she was. She had not eaten all day, had had only the water from the overflow pipe. The trip home—wherever that was—would take hours. "I spose I's always goin' to be hungry, may as well get used to it."

The auctioneer began his chant. She was finally sold to Mr. John A. Parrott for the sum of "one house, one lot, and one thousand dollars."

"Lordy mercy, dat man must think I's somebody special to pay dat much fo me. I wonders who he be." The man coming up the steps was the one with the big smile she had hoped would buy her. She almost squealed aloud.

Mr. Parrott led Hester to his buckboard, picked her up, and put her on the seat. He went around to the other side and climbed up by her. He didn't say a word but looked at her with a big friendly smile. Hester felt special just being by him.

Sitting up front like that, she could see where she was going. Mr. Parrott told her when they were close to "home." They passed a large green pasture with grazing goats, sheep, and cows. In one corner was a pond where the animals drank. Pigs were wallowing in the mud. On the pond wild ducks and white geese swam. How peaceful everything seemed.

Two possum hounds greeted them as they neared the Great House. They were running and barking as close to the horse's feet as they could without getting stepped on. The road in was lined with huge elms that almost met in the middle. As they rounded the curved driveway, Hester saw the house in front of them. Sitting on the edge of the seat, she exclaimed, "I declares, sur, dat be de purtiest, biggest white house I ever seen! Look how dat porch go all de way across de house and how dem big posts hold de roof up. It sho' would be nice to lie down in dat cool grass under dat old big tree." Hester was excited. As they came to the edge of the yard, a sweet fragrance like something from Heaven drifted from the running rose bush. Its pretty pink blossoms cascaded over the gate. She had a feeling everything was going to be all right now.

"Hester, how would you like to live in that big house?"

"Sur, I knows dat could never be. Dat too good to be true."

"Well, we'll see," Mr. Parrott replied.

Mrs. Eliza Parrott was waiting on the verandah to welcome her husband home. When Hester saw her, she thought, "Oh my, she smiling', lookin' happy too." Mrs. Parrott's skin was smooth as silk. Her cheeks were rosy, and she had eyes as blue as the sky. Her blond hair was pulled back and tucked into a net. "What a pretty lady. Her must be Missus Parrott. Her smilin' and happy to see us. Maybe she will like me. I sho hope she do."

Seeing Mr. Parrott give Mrs. Parrott a kiss on the cheek made Hester believe they were good, loving people. The lady took Hester by the hand and led her into the largest room Hester had ever seen. The wooden floor felt smooth and cool to her bare feet. She slid her foot on it, and, sure enough, there was no dust. She had never seen a winding stairway before. She couldn't speak. The only house she had been in was a one-room cabin with a dirt floor.

After turning the horse and buckboard over to a slave, Mr. Parrott joined his wife and Hester. He called out, "Mary, come down here a minute."

Hester watched "Miz Mary" come skipping down the

stairway. Her eyes were blue as a robin's eggs. Her blue gingham dress gathered over a crinoline underskirt made from stiff netting. It moved back and forth as she came down the steps, her blond curls bouncing.

Picking his daughter up and swinging her around, Mr. Parrott said, "Mary, I brought you a present from town."

"What, Daddy, *what?*"

"Not *what* Mary, but *who*," he replied. "This is Hester. She's your present. She belongs to you."

"I belong to dis purty girl, and I'll live in dis purty house," Hester thought. "Ma, you must uv sent an angel from Heaven to look atter me." There was no way she could hide her excitement. She shouted, "Hallelujah!"

"Don't get too excited, little girl," Mr. Parrott said, laughing. "You're going to have to work. You belong to Mary, and you will be doing things for her. You must clean the parlor, the children's room, and your room and help care for the children."

Hester thought, "Dat sound like a lot a work, but it will better dan bein' in dat hot sun in de cotton field.[10] And to live in dis

---

[10]Cotton was a demanding crop. After the seeds, planted in "hillocks," grew into cotton, the slaves spent many hours in hot, humid weather using a hoe to chop out the weeds that plagued in a time before pesticides. If these were too close to the plants, they had to bend over and pull them by hand. They couldn't stop work until the overseer blew his whistle, usually at dark but sometimes later if the moon

purty house wit dis purty girl, why, who could ask for mo? But what if I can't do de job?"

"Hester, welcome to our house. Come, let's go up to my room."

Hester hesitated as Mary started up the stairs. Not knowing what to do, she slowly took one step then another, all the while trying to hide her faded shirt, which was in a bundle under her arm. Halfway up, Hester stopped and looked over the banister railing. She saw a huge chandelier. It sparkled with color when Mr. Parrott opened the heavy front door and let in the afternoon sun. A big mirror hung on the wall reflecting a beautiful rose-colored velvet love seat that sat next to the stairway. She couldn't believe anyone could live in a place so pretty. At the top of the steps was a hallway with doors opening into more rooms. "I wonders what behind dem doors?"

Mary couldn't understand why Hester was curious about everything. She didn't realize the girl had never seen a house like this. Hester wanted to know about everything. In the

---

was bright. When the crop "ripened," generally in August, they pulled the soft, squashy cotton out of the hard, prickly-edged bolls that sometimes caused their fingers to bleed. Hanging over their shoulders was a long "gurney bag" they dragged beside them and stuffed with cotton. It normally held a hundred pounds. The slaves were given two ounces of cotton each. The women, after removed any seeds by hand, wove it on a spinning wheel to make a coarse fabric used for clothes and mattress covers, which were then filled with straw.

Hester

hallway were portraits hanging on the walls. Even Mary had no idea who they all were. Down the hall were beautiful tables with vases of fresh flowers and large upholstered chairs. Hester didn't even know what a chair was. Mary had a lot of teaching and explaining to do for this poor slave girl who had never had anything, scarcely even a family.

Hester

Chapter 7

Hester's and Mary's Rooms

Hester stood in the doorway, almost afraid to set foot in Mary's room for fear it would disappear and be a dream. She walked to the huge bed with tall posts and handmade crocheted canopy, gently moved her fingers across the soft spread and touched the mass of pillows at its head. She stood there enjoying and admiring something she had never experienced or seen before.

Pointing to a chest of drawers, Hester asked, "What dat fo?"

"I'll show you, Hester." Mary opened a drawer and revealed neatly placed crinolines, slips, and what she called "pantaloons." Another drawer held nightgowns. Mary showed her one. The long skirt was gathered onto the bodice. Lace was around the neck and at the bottom of the sleeves. Hester had never had a dress, much less a nightgown.

Over by the windows, with their lace and ruffled curtains, stood a table with books, a vase of flowers, and a kerosene lamp. Pink roses were painted on the lampshade. In the corner by the fireplace stood an oak washstand with a bowl and a pitcher of water. On another wall was a dresser with a mirror. Hester glanced in the mirror. What she saw frightened her, and she jumped back. "Who dat in dere, Missy Mary?"

"In where, Hester?"

Hester pointed to the mirror.

"That's you in the mirror, Hester."

"How I get in dere?"

"Hester, that's a mirror. It is just a reflection of you."

Hester cautiously went back to the dresser and looked in the mirror. She was shocked at what she saw. A small black face with piercing brown eyes and a head of little plaits all over it gazed back at her. This was the first time she had ever seen her image. She put her finger on the mirror and traced her face.

Under the bed was a bowl-like container with a lid. "What dat?"

"That is where you . . . relieve yourself if you have to go to the . . . toilet. You know."

"You means you dasn't hav to go outdoors for dat? Oh lordy

me!"

Slowly, Hester opened a door to the large wardrobe. "Oh lordy, oh lordy, do all dem dresses belongs to you, Missy Mary?"

"Yes they do. Don't you have dresses, Hester?"

Hester dropped her head and didn't answer.

"Hester, come see *your* room."

"*My* room! A room jist fo me?"

"Yes, just for you, Hester."

It was a small room adjoining Mary's. When she walked through the door, she was speechless. She had a little bed with a pillow, soft white sheets, and a quilt. She also had a washstand with a bowl and pitcher. She ran to the window and looked out. In the yard below was a large swing set in the middle of a mass of little flowers. The blue violets, yellow and purple crocuses, and hyacinths looked as though they rained from heaven. They were scattered over the yard. The Japanese quince was in full bloom, and daffodils lined the white picket fence. A soft breeze came through the window. Hester could almost taste the fresh air.

In her room was also a dresser with a "looking glass" and drawers. After looking to see if she was the same as in Mary's mirror, she hung her one faded shirt in the wardrobe but had nothing to put in the drawers.

"Don't worry, Hester. Mama will get you some clothes. For now, I'll let you have two of my older gingham dresses, some slips, pantaloons, and a gown. I may even have a pair of shoes you can wear."

Mary found Hester the items. It didn't matter if the shoes cramped her toes a little bit. She was used to that.[11] Hester had never had any underclothes and certainly not pantaloons. She ran into her room, hung the dresses in her wardrobe, and put the other clothes in her dresser drawers and the shoes in the bottom of the wardrobe. She was excited. She kept going back to the wardrobe touching the dresses as though she didn't believe they were there. She took out the nightgown. It had lace on the neck and sleeves and a long skirt. "Missy Mary, I's so happy you kind to me. At dem udder two plantations, dem people in the Great House never spekes to me."

Mary told Hester goodnight and went back to her room.

Hester poured water into her basin and, with a soft cloth and sweet-smelling soap, bathed herself. Burying her nose in the

---

[11]Slaves were allowed one pair of stiff, uncomfortable shoes annually made by their fellows on the plantation. Children grew quickly, and their toes cramped if the shoes lasted that long. They tied them together with strings until they were worn out completely, then went barefoot, even in snow. If they had no shoes during the winter, their feet cracked and bled, and the blood could be used to track them.

gown, she smelled its clean. After pulling it over her head, she stood in front of the mirror and turned around and around admiring herself.

She stood beside the bed for several minutes before she pulled the covers back. Gently, she ran her hands over the snow-white sheets, patted the pillow, and leaned over and smelled it. "It sho don't smell like dem nasty old rags I sleep on at Josephine house." She sat on the side of the bed and finally turned and slipped her feet between the smooth, soft sheets and put her head down on the pillow. "I thinks I's died and gone to Heaven. Ma, can you believe dis? I's really goin' to have a bed to sleep in instead of rags on de floor. I has a good home, nice people, and, best of all, a good friend." She sat up, bounced up and down on the bed, and got the silly giggles. She was so happy.

Hester pondered what had happened that day. It didn't seem so bad. The ride to the Parrott Plantation was pleasant. She'd been in front with Mr. Parrott, who had smiled and talked to her. So had Mrs. Parrott and Mary. With them and in their beautiful house, everything seemed good for the first time in her life. Tears of happiness sprang up. She didn't want them splashing onto her pretty gown and wiped them away with the bath towel. This was the first time she had cried for happiness instead of sadness. "I really believes my life gonna be different."

Slipping from her bed, Hester tiptoed to Mary's room, went over beside the bed, and stood looking at the beautiful girl with her blond curls spread out on the pillow. She sat by the window, saw cabins in the distance. The moon was shining bright, and farmland stretched out into the darkness. How happy she was she didn't have to live in a cabin again. A cool breeze came in through the window, blowing softly across her cheek. She peeped at Mary one more time and then returned to her room. Slipping back into her bed, she realized how tired she was. So much had happened to her that day. She fell asleep and slept until morning.

Chapter 8

Hester's New Life

Early next morning, Hester slipped out of bed and blinked her eyes several times just to make sure she wasn't dreaming. Looking in the mirror, she was relieved to find her reflection still there.

Slowly she opened the wardrobe. Miss Mary's dresses were there, too. Selecting the one she wanted to wear, she stood for a moment admiring it, then ran her hands over it, pressed her nose into the fabric, and placed it on the bed. At the dresser she took out a pair of pantaloons and a petticoat. Sitting on the bed, she held the pantaloons up, turned them this way and the other trying to decide what to do with them. She had never seen any clothing like them. She figured they had to go over her feet and up her legs because, other than the top, there were two openings. She put a foot through each hole, pulled them up, but, once on, they just didn't feel right. Finally, she realized she had them on backwards. Hester didn't bother with a petticoat but slipped the dress over her head. Standing in front of the mirror, she rubbed her hands down the front of the smooth, soft material.

Tiptoeing to Mary's room, she peeped in. Mary was asleep. As quietly as she could, she lit the fat lightwood under the oak in the fireplace. The flames, soon orange and blue, took the chill from the room. Hester poured warm water from the iron kettle that one of the housemaids had put in the hot coals the night before to stay warm until morning. She had seen Bessie do this many times. She laid out the soap and a bath cloth and towel.

Gently patting Mary on the shoulder, Hester said, "Missy Mary, don't you thinks you best gets up and dress? You said we eats breakfast after you has yo bath, and I's hungry."

"Hester, please make up my bed while I'm dressing. You're *my* maid now, remember."

"Missy Mary, I doesn't know how, but I will try." Hester walked to the bed and looked at it, wondering how to start. "How in de world do I makes up dis bed? Ain't never done sich afore." The extra pillows were on a chair by the bed. She worked and worked. The harder she tried, the worse matters got. The bed mattress was made from goose down. There had to be a special secret to making it look smooth, and she didn't know what it was. It looked like a big heap of lumps. She was almost in tears. "Maybe if I puts dese big pillows on de bed, it look better."

After Mary finished dressing, the two girls walked side by side down the long stairway. On entering the breakfast room, Hester thought the sunshine must live there. The walls were a soft yellow, and the vase of daffodils made it more cheerful. "I ain't ever seen such a bright, pretty room. Make me feel plumb happy. I jist believes everything gonna work out good fo me—maybe."

Sarah, the slave who served the family, gave Hester a handful of silverware and said, "Hester, place dese here on de table for de childrens."

Hester stood looking at the utensils, shook her head, then laid them on the table.

"Git to it, girl. Set dat table! What de matter wit you?"

"Ma'am, I ain't knowin' how to set no table. I's never seen dis kind of things before." She picked the utensils up, stood looking at them.

"Well, pay 'tention, girl, and I's show you how. The fok and napkin goes on de left side of dat plate. The knife go on de right. De spoon go side ov de knife. After dey finishes eatin', you comes eat in de kitchen."

As Hester took the dishes of food into the breakfast area for the smaller children of the household, she could barely stand it. She didn't know what all of it was, but she had never known anything to smell so good. The country ham cooking was nothing like greasy fatback. What could it be? The biscuits baking were the same way. She knew they had to taste good.

After she finished serving the children, she went into the kitchen, sat at a little round table, and enjoyed ham, eggs, grits, and homemade biscuits with strawberry jam. She also had a glass of milk. "Dat the bestest meal I ever et. I knows I ain't gonna be hungry no more."

After breakfast, Martha, another slave, called Hester to come with her. She was to teach her how to do her cleaning job. Hester thought each room was more beautiful than the last.

When they got to Mary's room and Martha saw Mary's bed, she scolded Hester. "Dat bed terrible! It look like a pile o' lumps!"

"Ma'am, I did de best I could. I work so hard, but I jist can't make it do right."

"Come on, young-un. I shows you how. Dere's a special way to do it. You has to fluff de feathers in dat mattress. Den you takes dis here stick and smooths it down by rubbin' it over de top until dere ain't no lumps. You don't wad dem sheets up under the bedspread. You pull 'em up smooth over the mattress, den pull de bedspread up. Now you puts de pillows at de head of de bed. Does you see, Hester?"

"Yassum. I tries to do better. I jist ain't know how." It took her quite a while to master the bed, but Martha was finally satisfied with it. Hester felt she would get better with time.

Martha took Hester into the parlor to dust the furniture and went about her duties. Hester turned around and around looking at the beautiful room. Over the fireplace mantle hung a large portrait of Mr. Parrott. He was very handsome. It seemed to Hester his eyes followed her as she walked to the other side of the room to smell the flowers on the table at the end of the sofa.

"What in de world dat thing by de wall?" She decided she would begin there. As she was dusting the keys of the piano, she accidentally pressed down on one. It startled her so much, she jumped backwards, bumped into a chair, fell over the arm, and tumbled topsy-turvy onto the floor. After collecting herself and smoothing her dress, she walked back to the piano and with a finger pressed one key and then another. She was amazed at the sound. Each key made a different noise.

Martha came running into the room. "Hester, what's you doin'? Don't you dare mess wid dat pinano! You quit messin' 'round and gets yo work done. Does you hear me?"

At night, Mary and Hester sat at the little table in Mary's room. By lamplight, Mary read to her.

"Missy Mary, does you think I will ever larn to read likes dat?"

"Of course you will, Hester. We'll find time, and I will help you. But we will have to keep it a secret. On most plantations, slaves are forbidden to learn to read and write."

Hester wondered if she could do all that was expected of her. She felt they maybe wanted too much from her. Each day was busy, held more for her to learn. She'd crawl into bed and fall asleep before she could finish her prayers.

Chapter 9

A Special Time for Mary and Hester

The next morning after Hester finished her chores and Mary her lessons, she said to Mary, "Let's go sit in dat swing I sees outen my window."

"That's a good idea, Hester."

Hester and Mary sat side by side. As they pushed with their toes, the swing went back and forth.

"Missy Mary, I's glad yo pa bought me, causin' de masters I had before be bad. Ma and me, we live in a log cabin wit other slaves. Hit made outen logs chinked wit mud. It be clay and water put together. Dey put dat mud 'tween de logs. When it dry, it sposed to keep out cold air. Don't work all de time. De chimney outta sticks and mud. Sometimes hit caught fire and have to be pull away to keep de whole cabin from a-burnin'. De floors all dirt."

"Hester, was the cabin dark? Did it have windows?"

"It sho dark. Have one winder an a door. Had to keep de shutter closed on dat winder to keep out all dat cole air. De room smoky 'cause usins cook in de fireplace."

"You're always talking about lye soap, Hester. How did your folks make it?"

"Ma put grease in de big iron pot what had fire under it. She pour lye in de grease, stir it wit a wood paddle. She pour in warter to make dat grease real thick. After it git cold, she cut it into chunks wit a knife. I 'member Ma tellin' 'bout a little boy ate some of dat lye one time. Kilt him daid. It won't all bad, dough. On Sunday nights, Ma puts grease on my hair. She taken up little sprigs of hair and wrap 'em from my scalp to the end wit string. She had it so tight, Missy Mary, dat the next morning I had festers. My scalp bad sore. I wear it like dat til Saddy night. Ma take de string off and wash my hair wit dat lye soap and comb it out. It felt so good, and hit was a pretty head of hair I had den."

"You didn't wash your hair all week, Hester? Didn't it smell bad with that grease in it?"

"It sho' do, but Ma ain't have no time to wash it durin' de week."

Hester told Mary her parents met at church. "Ma say, 'I knowed from de first time I lay eyes on him, I lovin' him. De way we got married was jumpin' de broom.'"

"Did they live on your mother's plantation or your father's, Hester?"

"After dey marry up, Pa still had to slip to Ma's cabin. If he'd a got caught, deyed a whipped him 'bout to death."

The sun was bearing down and making the girls too warm. "Missy Mary, it gettin' plum hot. Let's find a cooler place. Let's go lie down in dat cool green grass under dat big old shade tree. I's wanted to do dat all my life." When they reached the tree, they sat down. Then Hester stretched out on her stomach and smelled the green grass. It was as nice as she had imagined it would be.

Soon tiring of being so still, the girls went under the Great House, which sat on huge blocks of wood. Hester showed Mary little holes in the sand that looked upside-down. The big part was at the top, and went down to a point. "Now watch me, Missy Mary." Putting one end of a straw in the center of a hole, Hester twirled it around and sang, "'Doodle Bug, Doodle Bug, don't go away. Doodle Bug, Doodle Bug, come out and play.' Look, Missy Mary! Does you see dat fat little gray bug? He come out to see what goin' on."

Mrs. Parrott couldn't find the girls. They heard her calling, and Hester was afraid.

"Lordy mercy, Missy Mary, your ma skin me alive when she find us. Look how dirty we is."

Mary answered. "Here we are, Mama. Under the house." They crawled out. Mary's face and hands were smut black from the dust and dirt. Their clothes were filthy. Hester's face was ashen from the dust—and from being afraid she would get a whipping.

"Good gracious! Just look at the two of you! What were you doing under the house?"

"We've been finding doodlebugs, and it was fun!"

"Hester, I should whip you good. I know you put Mary up to that. The two of you get in that house and wash up! It's time for dinner."

Because she had never had a whipping on this plantation, Hester didn't know how bad it would be. She was thankful when she just received a scolding. Mary later told her that Mrs. Parrott would have used a peach tree switch and done the switching herself.

Sometimes when Mrs. Parrott found Hester spending too

much time with Mary and not doing her chores, she scolded her. Hester was not allowed to go to the cabins and play with the slave children, though, so Mrs. Parrott knew she was lonely and was glad that Hester and Mary were friends.

Hester Pearsall,
Former Slave

Hester's mother Carol belonged to "Mr. Bishop." Her father Sainty lived on another plantation, and she never knew his last name. She had a brother, William, but did not see him or her father again after Mr. Bishop sold her on the auction block in Kenansville, North Carolina, to "Mr. Miller." Some five years later, he sold her, also in Kenansville, to Mr. John A. Parrott, who lived near Kinston.

Hester at a much younger age, probably when she was working in Wilmington, North Carolina

Hester feeding the chickens on the day she was interviewed by Maude Pickett Smith (May, 1951)

Hester with Mrs. Eugenia Farmer, whose children she tended in Wilmington, North Carolina (c. 1902)

Hester with one of the Farmer children

Hester Pearsall in 1951 when Maude Pickett Smith interviewed her

Hester

Hester (date unknown)
Picture sent to Maude Pickett Smith by Alice Farmer Davis, granddaughter
of William and Eugenia Farmer, of Wilmington, North Carolina, for whom
Hester worked

Chapter 10

A Trip to Town

Needing supplies, Mrs. Parrott asked Roscoe to hitch a horse to the buggy and pick her up at the front door. Mary begged that she and Hester be allowed to go on the all-day trip to town and back.

"Has Hester finished her chores?"

"She's done most of them, Mama. Can't she miss doing the others this one time?"

"Well, I suppose so, just this once, mind you."

Hester and Mary flew out the door and climbed into the buggy before Roscoe could help them. They were impatiently waiting and wishing Mrs. Parrott would hurry so they could get started on their trip.

Mrs. Parrott came out at last, and Roscoe helped her into the buggy, climbed onto the seat up front, and said, "Giddy-up, hoss!"

Hester and Mary were so excited they got the silly giggles.

Mrs. Parrott warned them, "If you two don't settle down, I will take you back to the plantation."

It was a long trip, but they enjoyed looking at the many things along the way. Hester was thankful they didn't see any slaves being marched off to the slave market.

On arriving in Stricklandsville,[12] Hester noticed the tall elms with their limbs almost meeting in the middle of the street. The magnolias had beautiful large white blooms and waxy green leaves. Horses were hitched to the hitching posts on each side of the streets, which were lined with large, unpainted wooden buildings. Most had porches out front with benches where men visited and shared the news. Across the street from the General Store was a two-story hotel. Mrs. Parrott said it was among the oldest buildings in town and that people bringing their wares to be shipped by train usually spent the night there.

Roscoe pulled the horse up to a hitching post and tied the lines to the hook on it. While helping them down from the buggy, he told the girls, "Once when I to town, a hoss tied to one dem hitching posts got struck by lightnin' and kilt daid."

"Ooooooo, that was terrible," chimed Mary and Hester.

Under her breath, Hester thought, "I sho do hope ain't no

---

[12]Stricklandsville was the former name of Magnolia, North Carolina.

Hester

storm come up today 'causin if we has to stay in town in dat hotel, I won't have no place to sleep."

Hester had never been to town shopping. She was excited. She had heard of the General Store because some of the slaves gathered "Jerusalemote"[13] seed from the ditch banks at the plantation to dry and sent them to it by Roscoe. They were used for making medicine. To gather the seeds after they dried, they put cloth under the bushes and, with their hands around the spikes, rubbed the tiny brown seeds, causing them to fall on the cloth. They poured them into buckets to be sold or exchanged for supplies.

Hester and Mary followed Mrs. Parrott inside. The large doors were big and tall and looked round at the top. Mrs. Parrott pointed out the special molding on the door that made it appear "oval" and then explained what that meant. The brass knobs had lost their shine from people's handling. Hester thought it must take a giant key to unlock the doors.

When they were inside, Hester said, "Dem rooms at de plantation house big, but dis de biggest room I ever did see." For a few minutes, she hesitated to go on in. She felt she might be swallowed up.

---

[13]Jerusalem Oak.

That store[14] had anything a person could need or want. A long table down the middle was covered with pants, shirts, and other clothes for men. On the walls were shelves with boxes of shoes, fabric for dresses, curtains, thread, needles, and even food.

"Missy Mary, look at dem shoes! I didn't know you could buy shoes. I thought us slaves make 'em at de plantation. And look at all dat purty cloth for dresses! Missy Mary, what dat big round yellow thing in dat box?"

"That's cheese, Hester." Mary was kept busy explaining this and that and enjoyed "educating" Hester, who thought the coffee smelled good but quickly moved on to the jars of stick candy on the counter and didn't know what they were either. Mrs. Parrott told them they could have two sticks each.

"Oh my, I thinks I has dat one wit the white and red stripes and dat other wit white and yellow stripes." Hester was especially pleased when Mary chose the same. "Umm, dat candy sho be good. I's never had nothin' like dat, Missy Mary. Has you?"

"Yes, Papa always brings me some when he's been away on a trip, but I'm glad he brought you instead of candy the last time."

---

[14]For the history of the Newbury store and Magnolia's development as a bulb center, see Maude Pickett Smith, "H. E. Newbury," *The Heritage of Duplin County, North Carolina – 2012.* Wallace, NC: County Heritage, Inc. In press.

"I sho am glad of dat, too, Missy Mary."

While Mrs. Parrott was making her purchases, Hester and Mary continued through the store. In the back were burlap bags of salt, rice, sugar, and coffee. When they wandered into a separate room, the smell was something horrible. The fertilizer and seeds were stored there to keep the fertilizer odor from getting into the coffee and ruining it.

Finally, they went outside to find Roscoe.

"Missus Parrott, what dat beside de store?"

"Hester, that's a railroad track. Do you see the iron rails? A train has wheels that run on the track. It also has a large engine. Wood is put into the furnace to make fire. The fire boils the water in the boiler to make the steam that moves the train. People ride on trains."

Hester was excited. She ran over and touched the iron railing and looked up and down it, hoping to see a train coming. "Oh my, Missus Parrott, I sho wishes I could see one of dem trains, and I hopes I can ride on one of 'em."

"Hester, people do more than *ride* the train. This very railroad track you're looking at is the longest in the world—one hundred and sixty-one miles long. It runs from Wilmington, which you've heard talked of, to Weldon, a town in the southeastern part of our state of North Carolina. People come here from long distances to ship their tobacco, turpentine, cotton, flower bulbs, and other wares and goods. And to get things that come here by train, too."

Hester was hoping they'd wait long enough to see a train, but Mrs. Parrott thought they should begin their trip home. Hester wondered if she would ever see a train.

Chapter 11
Hester the Teenager

Hester had been with Mr. and Mrs. Parrott and Mary three years and was now thirteen and took great pride in her work. Martha, the slave who taught her how to do her chores, was pleased with Hester's learning ability and knew that she went about her work with a song in her heart. Now when Hester fluffed the feather mattress and smoothed it with a stick, it looked as good as if Martha had prepared it. Hester wished all slaves could be lucky enough to have a good home and a master who cared about his slaves.

But changes were coming. Mary and her friends exchanged dances, birthday parties, and other social events. Her interests were no longer centered on Hester, who knew that she was still a slave.

One Saturday afternoon while Mary was at her friend's house across the creek for a party, Hester sat by her bedroom window and looked out at the slave quarters. Children were running about in their yards. Some boys pushed a metal rim with a stick. Others played tag or acted out stories with dolls. Hester remembered her mother making her a doll from a corncob. Carol had wrapped cloth around the cob for a shirt and used straw for the hair, which was held on with a little bandana made from a scrap of cloth. Hester had had to play with the other slave children before coming to the Parrott house, and now she wasn't allowed to go to their quarters. She was envious of them but thankful that they could play on Saturdays when Mr. Parrott let them and their parents have the day to do things for themselves, so long as the tools were ready for use on Monday morning.

Mr. Parrott provided a space for a family to have a small vegetable garden, and the children kept out the animals. He also gave each one a pig, which they kept in a six-foot-square pen made from small logs. The pigs were fed "slops" or scraps from the table. In the winter was "hog killing." For the Great House, the slaves killed and prepared sometimes as many as thirty hogs. The meat was packed down in salt to keep it from spoiling. Hester closed her eyes and put her hands over her ears so she couldn't hear the squeals when the hogs were hit in the head with the killing axe. Sometimes, Hester slipped away to the hog killing and used a forked stick to spear a piece of liver from the large iron pot where it was cooking and pulled a sweet potato from the hot ashes, peeled it, and ate it with the liver.

Although Hester was happy, she sometimes wished she could visit the slave children at their play. "Maybe today be a good day to go. Missy Mary gone and won't know I's been." Her mind was made up. Cautiously, she crept down the stairs and out the back door, knowing anyone seeing her would think she was going to the garden. When she arrived, the children quit what they were doing and stood starring at her. They had never seen her before and were a little afraid. She saw a boy she felt was about the age of her brother, William. She walked to him, gently put her hand on his shoulder, and asked: "Son, what yo name?"

With his head bowed, he shyly replied, "Mah name Jeremiah."

"Jeremiah, is you happy here with Marse Parrott?"

"Yasam, I's happy."

She wondered if her brother was at a place where he could be happy.

Hester didn't tarry long for fear she'd be missed. She scurried back to the Great House and went to her room. She thought about Bessie, Josephine, William, and her father Sainty, wondering if they had been sold, too. She missed them very much.

When Mary came home from the birthday party, she told

Hester about the homemade ice cream and birthday cake and the good time she'd had. Hester visualized them and could almost taste the food. She thought, "Maybe when Missy Mary have her birthday, she lets me have some cake." She didn't tell Mary she had been to the slave yard. That was her secret.

Chapter 12

Christmas at the Parrott Plantation

"Missy Mary, can you believe only fo mo days to Christmas?"

"My goodness, Hester, there is a lot to be done around the Parrott Plantation before that. We'd better get busy."

Christmas at the plantation was celebrated December 25th until New Year's. Hester envisioned the table of foods grown, hunted, and prepared by the slaves—turkey, ham, quail, dressing, rice, giblet gravy, collards, butterbeans, corn, pickled peaches, cornbread, and biscuits. On the sideboard would be mincemeat, sweet potato and apple pies, plus ambrosia with whipped cream and cakes galore. As they worked, Martha and Sarah sang carols heard throughout the house, but nobody shushed them.

"Papa, won't you please go with Hester and me to find a Christmas tree?" It was an important symbol at the Parrott house, and the girls were eager to find just the right one.

"I'll go, but you must put on warm clothes. It's very cold."

Mary let her use a pair of her mittens, which made Hester's hands clumsy, and a toboggan that felt warm on her head and ears. They searched and searched and discarded several after discovering missing branches. Finally all agreed that they had the perfect one for the parlor. Mr. Parrott chopped it down at ground level with his axe and pulled it across the field to the Great House. Hester and Mary frolicked, skipped, tagged each other, or ran in circles around him. The dragging bruised the cedar and let out its smell, which put excitement and Christmas magic in the air. Christmas was here! When they arrived, Mr. Parrott asked Roscoe to nail the tree to boards to make it stand straight and tall.

"Ain't dat de prettiest tree you ever see, Missy Mary? It gonna be de best we ever have. I's so happy, I could almost cry. Roscoe, you make dat tree straight. We ain't having no junk around here dis Christmas." The girls watched as Roscoe took it into the parlor and placed it in the corner by the fireplace.

That night, Mary's parents joined the girls in the parlor. They enjoyed hot chocolate and cookies. Mr. Parrott popped corn over the coals of the fire using a covered container with a long handle, then put on another log. Hester and Mary sat on the floor as Mrs. Parrott threaded their needles for them to make strings of popcorn decorations, adding, "Girls, I bought red ribbon for bows for the tree."

Mr. Parrott said, "Girls, I have a surprise for you also. When I was in town last week I bought something for our tree." It was a beautiful angel with porcelain head and hands and a ruffled dress. He lifted Mary to place her at the tree's top. Gold wings extended from each side, rising above her head. They glittered and sparkled in the light from the fireplace and lamps. The girls were delighted.

"Dat be de prettiest thing I's ever seen, Missy Mary, but what be it?"

"An angel, Hester. When Jesus was born, angels appeared from heaven and sang 'Glory to God on the Highest.' They were announcing the birth of Jesus. Christmas celebrates His birthday."

"Oh lordy, Missy Mary, I never heard dat before, but I likes it. I knows God sent Baby Jesus to earth so he could tell us about our Heavenly Father, God."

On Christmas Eve morning after Hester did her chores, she and Mary went outside to gather holly branches, shiny green Magnolia leaves, and cedar. A deep snow had fallen during the night, and they had to throw snowballs at each other and tumble in it.

They put holly on the mantels in all the bedrooms, other greenery in the parlor, and Magnolia leaves on the dining room mantel, buffet, and table, adding red bows where appropriate. Martha placed red candles in pewter candlesticks, all made on the plantation, on the buffet and table.

Roscoe cut a large bunch of mistletoe growing in the big oak tree and brought it to Mrs. Parrott. She tied a red ribbon on it, and Mr. Parrott hung it from the hall chandelier. Hester and Mary watched from the parlor as Mrs. Parrott stepped under the mistletoe, and her husband kissed her.[15] The teenagers put their hands over their mouths and giggled. They wouldn't dare be seen being kissed. In fact, Hester didn't remember ever being kissed by anyone.

On Christmas Eve, stockings were hung on each mantle in the children's bedrooms. In the morning, they rushed over to find them filled with such items as toy horns, balls, pocket knives for those old enough, cars, dolls . . . . The girls might also get music boxes and jewelry. Everyone had apples, oranges, nuts, and candy.

After the family finished eating breakfast, Mrs. Parrott asked Roscoe to bring the children from the slave quarters. Each was

---

[15]Standing under the mistletoe gave a person "permission" to kiss you.

given a hearty breakfast, including milk, and fruit and sticks of candy. Hester enjoyed being with them, and her heart swelled with pride to see the Parrotts caring for the slave children. She wished she'd had a childhood with a good master and wondered if William had.

After dinner, everyone in the household met in the parlor. Mrs. Parrott played Christmas carols on the piano, and they all sang together. After Mr. Parrott read the Christmas story, they exchanged and opened gifts. Mary gave Hester one wrapped in shiny red paper with a gold bow on top. "Hester, this is for you. You have helped me so much this year; I wanted to do something nice for you."

Hester's hands were shaking. She had never had a gift. She carefully pulled the bow and ribbon off, placing them on the floor, then pulled the paper off the package. When she slowly opened the box and lifted the tissue paper, she found something bright on a bed of cotton—a gold chain with a shiny gold cross. This was the first real Christmas gift Hester had ever received, and she had never owned any jewelry. Running to Missy Mary, she got down on her knees, and, with tears streaming, looked up at Mary, who fastened the necklace around her neck. "Missy Mary, thank you, thank you, from the bottom of my heart! I will never take dis pretty necklace off. I's sorry, but I don't has you no gift. I didn't have no way to get you one."

"That's all right, Hester. I didn't expect you to give me a gift. You enjoy the gift I gave you. I am happy you like it."

In late afternoon, friends from surrounding plantations came to the Parrott house. A group played music. Hester couldn't join them, but she sat on the stairs and watched the men in what Mary said was "formal dress" and the women wearing shades of gold, blue, red, green, and purple. They danced the waltz again and again. Afterwards, Mrs. Parrott played the piano, and the guests sang carols.

The slaves decorated their cabins with holly, cedar, and berries and ate ham, rabbit, squirrels, and quail, along with vegetables they had preserved from their gardens. They got together and celebrated Christmas with songs and were given three days off from working the fields.

Chapter 13

Trying Times

"Hester, guess what? Today's my fifteenth birthday. Would you like to help with my party?"

"Oh yes, I sho' would, Missy Mary. I hopin' you aks me to help. Dat make me happy. I go see if Sarah has de cake ready. Can you git de napkins, plates, an silverware? We needs fresh flowers for the table and house. We want it to look pretty, don't us, Missy Mary?"

"Yes, we do, Hester. We have to get the punch bowl and cups out and have Sarah wash them. Has she made the ice cream yet?"

"I'll check and see, Missy Mary."

Hester and Mary finished getting the preparations ready for the party, and Mary had to dress because her guests would soon be arriving. The buggies began pulling up in front of the house.

The girls were wearing lovely party dresses, but no one would be as beautiful as Hester's Missy Mary. Her blue taffeta dress matched her eyes perfectly. Her blond hair was pulled back in a bunch of curls, and ringlets framed her face. The guests entered the dining room where Mary welcomed them and thanked them for coming. Using a silver ladle, Hester poured punch from the cut glass bowl into crystal cups. Sarah brought out a large cake with white icing, pink roses, green leaves, and fifteen pink flaming candles. Mary leaned over and blew hard but didn't quite extinguish them all, so Hester stepped up to blow the rest out. Everyone sang, "Happy Birthday, Dear Mary."

Mary had a surprise for Hester. Even though no one know her exact birthday, the Parrotts guessed Hester might be about her age. She served Hester a piece of birthday cake and a dish of ice cream and sang "Happy Birthday, Hester!" The others joined in. Hester realized that Missy Mary had deliberately left her some candles to blow out.

Hester, poking her lips out and mumbling to herself, helped Martha clean up the dishes. Since Missy Mary let her celebrate her birthday with cake and ice cream, she thought she would let her join them in the parlor to see the gifts opened. No matter how special her day had been, she was just a slave and couldn't

Hester

be included in Mary's circle of friends.

The dinner table that night was completely quiet. Why weren't they excited about Missy Mary's birthday? After they went to their rooms, Hester asked, "Missy Mary, what wrong? Nobody happy tonight. It make me sad."

"Hester, I noticed that, too. I don't know. I wanted to ask Mama but was afraid to. I believe she will tell me in her own time."

The next morning at breakfast, Hester noticed that the house slaves were also quiet. They didn't have much to say to her. Finally, Hester asked, "Martha, what de matter? Why everybody so quiet and acting funny?"

"Hester, dere be talk of war."

"What dat?"

"I can't say no more now, Hester. Jist be quiet."

That night when she got to her room, Hester heard Mary crying and ran in to her. She had never seen Missy Mary so upset. "Missy Mary, what de matter? What wrong?"

"Hester, I'm not supposed to talk about this, but you are my friend, and I just have to tell you. There are rumors of a war."

"What is a war, Missy Mary?"

"Hester, a war is when two sides believe in different things.

They go out and kill each other until one side loses."

"Kill each other? I's never heard of sich a thing. People don't kill each other." Wringing her hands, Hester paced up and down. Finally she took Mary in her arms and tried to soothe her. In her mind, she saw men facing each other, screaming at the tops of their voices, and slashing each other with their whips. She cringed to think of such happenings.

After Mary calmed down a bit, she said, "Hester, if there is a war, the men will have to join the Army and leave home. You know I've been seeing Mister Brad Perkins. I like him a lot. What if he has to go off to war? What if Papa has to go to war? What will we do, Hester?"

"I don't know, Missy Mary, but I sho' will look after you and Missus Eliza. I promises."

Chapter 14
Hester Lonely

"Missy Mary, is you goin' out wit Young Mistah Brad agin?"

"Well, yes I am, Hester. Why do you ask? You know that, with war in the air, I wish to be with him all I can. We never know when he may be leaving."

"I just can't understand it," thought Hester. "Missy Mary have a boyfriend, and I can't even go to de slave quarters. I don't even know no boy. I's suppose to be de same age as Missy Mary. When is I suppose to git a boyfriend?" Hester loved Mary, but she was beginning to notice a big change in their relationship. She felt left out.

It was late afternoon when Brad came to see Mary. Hester stood at the window and watched them leave. She felt alone. In Mary's room, she tidied up things on the little round table.

Walking to Mary's wardrobe, she opened the door and slowly thumbed through her beautiful dresses. Hester had to wear a dark dress with a white apron over it and a white cloth tied around her head. Even when she went to church with the Parrotts, she removed the apron but wore a dark dress. At the church, she had to sit with the house servants in a special section of the "slave gallery." Hester was happy she had a good home with plenty of food and a bed to sleep in, but her thoughts went back to her mother, Carol; her brother, William; and her father, Sainty. She recalled all the bad things in her life and knew she should be happy and thankful, and she was. She was just lonely.

Hester had not heard much more about a war. She was happy for that and thought it was a rumor. "I wonders what dey to fight about anyways." She did not realize it was for her freedom and what a difference it would make in her life.

Mary didn't return home until around nine o'clock that night. Usually she told Hester where she was going and when she would be back, but this time she hadn't. Even when she returned, she had little to say. Hester took Mary's nightgown from the chest of drawers and put it on the chair by the washstand. Both girls were very quiet. After helping Mary get dressed for bed, she said, "Goodnight, Missy Mary, I hopes you had a nice time with Mistah Brad."

Mary said, "Thank you Hester," and slipped under the sheets. Hester tucked her in for the night.

Hester took her time getting ready for bed. After putting her gown on, she sat by her bedroom window and looked out. The moon was shining, and she could see silhouettes of the trees, land, and cabins. Sitting by this window had become her sanctuary where she could think. All was quiet except for the crickets chirping and the frogs croaking in the pond nearby. She wondered what was going on in other parts of the land, could not imagine. Looking out her bedroom window, she noticed a small group of slaves in a huddle outside a cabin. "I wonders what goin' on out dere. I's never seen dem do dat afore." Hester quietly slipped into Mary's room. She didn't want to awaken her, but she needed to talk to someone. She crept to Mary's bedside and peeped at her. Mary's eyes were closed, but she sensed Hester's presence and opened them. "Missy Mary, I's sorry. I ain't mean to wake you up, but now dat you is, I needs to talk wit you."

"What's the matter, Hester? Is something wrong?"

"I don't know, Missy Mary. I jist seen a bunch of slave men together talkin'. I's never seen dat before. Not dis time of night."

"I don't know, Hester. I'll ask Mama in the morning. Go to

bed and go to sleep. It will be all right."

Hester went back to her room but didn't get much sleep that miserable night. "If Missy Mary ain't wantin' to be 'round me anymore, I sho' sad." Finally, she watched the sun come up. It was time to get ready for breakfast. Maybe a good night's sleep had made Missy Mary the same as before.

Hester got Mary up and ready, and they went down for breakfast. When they arrived, Hester knew something was wrong. The house slaves were jittery and sad or frightened. Hester wasn't sure which.

"Martha, what de matter? Don't tell me nothing, causin' I knows better. Things jist ain't right."

"Hester, dat war talk real." Don't you say nothin' 'bout it, but de Noth and de South a-goin' to fight 'bout freein' us slaves."

"Oh, lordy, lordy! What in the world I do if us freed? I ain't got no family. I ain't got nobody but *dis* family. Where will I go? Where will I live? What will I do?" She was almost in tears. Martha told her to be quiet and get about her chores.

Later that morning, Hester heard a commotion in front of the Great House. She ran to the door and saw Young Mistah Brad Perkins running his horse like he was going to a fire. When he got to the steps, he jumped off and began calling Mary. His face was red and sweaty, and he looked as though he'd seen a ghost.

Mary came out to meet him. "Brad, what's wrong?"

"Mary, where is your father? Something terrible has happened. I need to talk with him. *Now!*"

Mary led him to the parlor. "Brad, my boy, what's the matter?"

"Mr. Parrott, we are at war!" Brad shouted. "Yesterday morning at 4.30 in Charleston, South Carolina, the South fired on Fort Sumter. They fought for thirty-three hours until the Union soldiers finally surrendered. I was in town, and everybody was talking about it.[16]

"What does it mean, Papa?"

"I'm not sure, Mary. We must wait and see."

Hester was standing in the doorway and heard the conversation. She was petrified. She wasn't sure she wanted to know more.

That night, Mr. Parrott called the family, Hester, and the house slaves into the parlor. He told them things looked bad, that a war between the states had begun. The young men would have to join the Army and would be leaving. He wasn't sure if he would have to go, but "our" side would need all the men they could get. "I hope all of you respect Mrs. Parrott and me enough

---

[16]Fort Sumter was attacked 13 April 1861.

to take care of her, Mary, and the little children if I do have to go. You know what your jobs are, and I expect you to carry them out."

Hester knew Missy Mary was heartbroken because Mister Brad would have to "go to war." She was almost glad she didn't have a "suitor." She stepped forward and said, "Marse Parrott, you knows I will do all I can to protect Missy Mary and Missus Eliza. You knows I loves dem. You is all de family I's got."

The next day, April 14, 1861, Hester watched men making their way to Kinston to join what was called "the Confederate Army." What a sad time it was. The men seemed excited. They were fighting to keep slavery and felt sure of winning the war. They were ready and anxious to go.

In a few days, Young Mistah Brad came to the Parrott Plantation to tell Mary he was leaving for the Army. The Confederates had defeated the Union Army at Fort Sumter, and he felt that he and the other young men could conquer the world.

Chapter 15

Devastation at the Parrott Plantation

"Roscoe, I hear you tellin' Martha and Sarah dere be Union soldiers in de area? Dat if deys fightin' in dat New Bern, deys nearby, too. What else you knows, Roscoe?"

"Dem Union soldiers cruel. Goin' from plantation to plantation stealin' everthing dey finds. Burnin' homes and barns."

"You knows dey ain't doing dat, Roscoe!"

"Dey fo sure is, Hester."

"Oh my. Oh my." Hester wrung her hands together. "Dat terrible."

Hester listened to whoever she could, tried to piece it together. The Union soldiers were called Yankees and came mostly from the North, where the people were wealthy because they had factories, shipping, and large businesses. Some people in the South were wealthy because they had large plantations, and a few dealt in shipping, but a lot of them had plantations and made their incomes on crops that depended on good growing seasons. Bad weather meant they had nothing to sell and had to wait and hope for a better season the next year.

Mr. Abraham Lincoln was elected President of the Union, which was also the North mostly, in 1860. There were eleven Southern states. They were the Confederate States of America or the Confederacy. Mr. Jefferson Davis became the President of it. Soldiers of the South fought for "states' rights," which were supposed to decide the future of slavery. The Union soldiers fought to put the country together again and free four million slaves.

The war was also called "Brother against Brother" because sometimes brothers came face to face in battle. This happened because the "border states" had a lot of people on the side of the North and a lot on the side of the South.

Hester still couldn't understand why the menfolk wanted to go to war. After it began, the Southern men were hot to volunteer, but when things became tough, they sent word home for their families and friends not to volunteer, which created a problem. Something known as the "Confederate Congress" called for, like, a 100,000 troops. Men 18 up to 35 had to "sign up" for three years. Later on, when things got so bad, the "draft" thing went from 17 to 50.

Hester wanted Marse John to stay home. Many Confederate soldiers were sick, wounded or killed, or ran away. Some soldiers slept in "tents," which a lot of them didn't have. If the ground was wet, they spread oilcloth and placed their blankets atop it. If it was raining, they had to put the oilcloth over their blankets. When winter came, it was very cold and sometimes snowed. Hester hoped Young Mistah Brad had a good place to sleep. She knew Missy Mary was worried about him. She would take him food if she knew where he was. The Southern boys didn't have enough clothing or food. Many were ill, and their ammunition was about gone. They suffered from frostbite, hunger, and sickness, especially "dysentery." Many died from that dysentery. Some died from war injuries. A lot got shot with "mini ball" bullets that shattered their bones and made them lose arms and legs or even killed them. There weren't many doctors or "surgical" tools. Sometimes they used saws to "amputate" arms and legs. There was little "anesthesia" to help with pain, and some were given whiskey or nothing. So-called hospitals were set up in plantation homes.

Mr. Parrott was "called up." He could have had Roscoe take

his place under the "substitute policy" but felt Roscoe would be more helpful at home. If necessary, Roscoe would take the family to the other Parrott plantation, which was farther off the main road. It was a sad time. Hester and the house slaves stood on the front porch with Mrs. Parrott and Mary and the other children as they waved to Mr. Parrott and the other men as long as they could see them. Some of the slaves were happy they might be freed but continued to be faithful to their master.

Even though she felt like crying herself, Hester said, "Missus Eliza, please don't cry. I'll take care of you while Marse John is gone. Lordy mercy, Missy Mary, I's heard the Yankees on the way here. We's got to hide things, causin' they will take everthing dey get dere hands on. I'll go tell Roscoe to take de cows and pigs into de swamp. Maybe dey can't find dem dere."

Hester pulled a coop way up under the house, and she and Mary chased chickens all over the yard, caught them, and put them in it. They added corn, hoping it would keep the chickens quiet. Martha put the silverware in the fireplace and covered it with wood. Hester and Mary hid in a closet. Mrs. Parrott was very frightened but believed she must stand up to the coming Yankees. She positioned herself under the chandelier, where mistletoe once hung, and waited for them.

The Yankees rode up on their spirited horses, tied them to the hitching post, dismounted, and came up the front steps. Pushing Mrs. Parrott aside, they plundered the house looking for anything they could find. They didn't want the china, so they smashed it. They meant to destroy everything, leaving the plantation with nothing of value. They swept any unwanted items off the sideboard onto the floor. They stuffed all the food they could find—hams, sausage, flour, rice, and cornmeal—into sacks and carried it away.

In the storage area outside, they found the barrel of molasses but couldn't take it, so they poured it onto the ground. One soldier stuck his finger in it and tasted it but didn't much like it. They took the one pig Roscoe was unable to get to the swamp.

Hester was upset. She heard the pig squealing but wasn't sure what was happening. Mary was sobbing, afraid for her mother. "Missy Mary, you stay in dis closet. I's gonna see about Missus Eliza." Just as Hester came down the stairs, a trooper grabbed Mrs. Parrott by an arm. Hester ran to the kitchen, picked up a piece of oak wood, ran into the hallway, and screamed at the man to leave her Missus Eliza alone.

"Now just what do you think you can do, little nigger?" He laughed at Hester, took the oak wood from her, and strolled out the door. Mrs. Parrott was much shaken. She, Hester, Mary, and Martha walked through the house assessing the damage. It was bad, but they were thankful they were alive and the house hadn't been burned.

Mrs. Parrott and Mary had never been responsible for taking care of things on the plantation. Mary didn't know how to catch chickens. "Hester, look at these scratches on my arms. What am I going to do? I don't know how to do these things. Why is this happening to us?"

"Don't you worry none, Missy Mary. I will doctor yo scratches." She rubbed healing ointment on the bad places and assured Mary she would have no scars. "I takes care of you and Missus Eliza. Oh, Lordy, look yonder, Missy Mary. Does you see that cloud of dust down de road? More Yankees comin', and we ain't got nothin' put up. Dey finish gettin' everthing fo sure."

Mary started looking for her mother. Hester ran to the kitchen squalling for Sarah and Martha and then to the barn for Roscoe. She was afraid she wouldn't have time to get word to everybody the Yankees were coming again.

Mrs. Parrott had sewn her jewelry to the crinoline under her dress. Sarah put what meat was left on a ledge in the fireplace chimney. They could always wash the smut off. Roscoe had gotten one of the cows, a calf, and the bull to the swamp, but there was still one cow in the barn.

The Yankees were coming up the drive. Mary ran upstairs and hid under her bed. Hester stayed to look after Mrs. Parrott.

Some of the soldiers rode their horses all over Mrs. Parrott's bed of red, white, yellow, and lavender roses fertilized with cow manure from the barn. They tore down the archway with the beautiful, sweet-smelling pink roses that met you as you entered the rose garden.

Roscoe later found out that some of the soldiers had come upon a whiskey still deep in the woods. He told Hester they probably didn't know it was made of corn and water with a little lye and cow manure thrown in. They got very drunk and set the barn and smoke house on fire. When the cow ran out, one of the Yankees shot her but didn't take any of the meat.

Others on this second raid came in the house, turned over furniture, and slashed the family portraits and Hester's mattress, scattering goose feathers everywhere. Luckily, when they didn't find any jewelry in it, they didn't bother to search the others. They broke Mary's pretty lamp shade with the roses painted on it and dumped the dresser drawers in all the bedrooms searching for valuables.

Again, a soldier grabbed Mrs. Parrott. He swung her around, and she was afraid she'd lose the baby she was carrying. Hester found a broom and went after him, shouting for him to leave her lady alone. He finally took the broom away from her and snatched her necklace with the cross that Mary had given her. It left a welt across the back of her neck. He pushed her down and ran out the door. Hester was dazed for a few minutes. Devastated that her necklace was gone, she screamed at the soldiers, who also took away Mrs. Parrott's beautiful horse. They didn't have too long to cry before discovering the out buildings set afire. They joined the slaves in carrying buckets of water but couldn't save the buildings.

Hester got Roscoe and some of the other slaves to butcher the cow. They took the meat to the cool cellar and salted it down. They were happy for the beef and the bit of food that was left. The small crocks of canned vegetables were broken. They did have some cabbage kraut in a barrel. It smelled bad, so the soldiers didn't want it. They still had eggs because the Yankees didn't find the chickens Hester hid under the house, and the sweet potatoes remained safe in their mound of dirt and pine straw that kept them from freezing in the winter. And they still had the cow and calf Roscoe had hidden in the swamp. Hester urged Mrs. Parrott to move to the other plantation.

They put the food, sheets, blankets, and the few remaining dishes and pots in the wagon. They had no horse, so Roscoe hooked the bull to it. He tied the cow to the back and let the calf follow its mama and had some of the slaves lead the pigs into the swamp and leave them. They loaded the coop with the chickens on the wagon, and, last, Mrs. Parrott, who couldn't walk that far because of being in a family way.

Hester looked back at the beautiful home they were leaving and was sad and also angry. She didn't want to go, and she especially didn't want to lead her master's old nurse. Mr. Parrott let her live at the plantation because she had nowhere to go. Hester was energetic and didn't want to poke along with that old woman. Letting her emotions get the best of her, she decided she wasn't going with the family. She turned and ran back towards the Great House. When she got to the top of the hill, two Yankee soldiers shot at her twice. She ran, jumped in the creek, and hid under the bridge.

Mrs. Parrott missed Hester, and they went back to look for her. Hester ran out to warn them, but it was too late. The soldiers rounded them up and took all of them back to the Great House, where Mrs. Parrott fainted and fell in a heap in the yard.

Hester ran to her, gathered her in her arms, all the while calling out, "Missus Eliza, Missus Eliza, please don't die!"

Mrs. Parrott roused enough to say, "Hester, everything is going to be all right. You take care of the children." The soldiers took her into the house and told Hester, Mary, and the others to stay on the porch. Hester was very upset and was convinced the soldiers were going to harm or kill Mrs. Parrott and that Mr. Parrott would be disappointed if he knew what she had done.

The soldiers later took them in the house and put Hester and the children in a room, locked the door, and told them to be quiet or they would be shot. A small amount of food was brought to them. The next afternoon, two soldiers came and led them up to Mrs. Parrott's bedroom. She was holding the baby boy she had delivered. She named him John.

Wounded soldiers were lying on the blood-stained rug in the Parrotts' parlor. The furniture was piled in a corner. Soldiers cried out in pain. Some begged for their mothers. Others prayed. A hospital was set up, and Hester helped care for them. She bathed their brows with cool cloths and gave them sips of water. She didn't care if they were Yankees. They needed care. She tore up the sheets for bandages, and they used up all the food. The Yankee soldiers stayed at the Parrott house for about two weeks until the war ended.[17]

Hester was around twenty years old. She was told that the South had lost the war, and the slaves would be freed. She didn't know what that meant exactly or what would happen next.

---

[17]9 April 1865.

Hester

Chapter 16

Homecoming

"Missy Mary! Missus Eliza! Everbody come quick! I sees horses and mens comin' down de road. Does you reckons it might be our Marse Parrott?"

Hester, Mary, Mrs. Parrott, and the house slaves stood on the front porch and steps watching and wondering. Hester and Mary ran down into the yard hoping to see for sure if it was Mr. Parrott.

"Look, Missy Mary, I does believe dat Marse John!"

"I don't know, Hester. That doesn't look like Papa. He's too thin."

As the men came nearer, one horse broke from the group and came towards the porch. The rider dismounted and looked at his family. He was devastated at what he saw—the barn and smoke house burned, the rose bed trampled, the crops destroyed . . . . But his family was alive!

Hester couldn't believe the man she'd known—tall, straight and with a twinkle in his eyes—was this thin, pale person with sad eyes and drooped shoulders. He walked slowly with a limp. She took Mrs. Parrott's arm. "Missus Eliza, it be Marse John. Come with me." Hester gently led her to her husband, who took his wife in his arms and held her close. Tears streamed down their faces. Mary slowly approached and put her arms around her parents. Mr. Parrott embraced her and patted Hester on the shoulder. Nobody was able to speak at that moment. Finally, Mrs. Parrott took her husband's hand and led him, Hester, and Mary to the house.

Hester knew she had a big job ahead. How would she ever be able to nurse Mr. Parrot back to good health when they had almost nothing left?

Mr. and Mrs. Parrott and Mary were in the parlor. Hester, Martha, and Sarah searched the kitchen to see what they could find to feed him. He drank the glass of milk Hester brought from the cellar as if starved.

"Sarah, I's found one old hen dem Yankees miss." Hester ran in one direction and Sarah in the other until they pinned her in the corner of a fence. She flapped her wings and struggled, but Hester finally managed to tuck her under an arm. She passed her to Sarah, who took the head and jerked and twisted until the neck was broken, then dipped her in boiling water and plucked the feathers.

"Sarah, you boil dat old chicken and make some broth for Marse Parrott. It give him strength."

"Papa, did you see Brad while you were gone? We haven't heard from him since he left for the army." Mary was very worried. Everyone was coming home from the war. Where was he?

"No, I haven't heard from him or seen him."

Mr. Parrott didn't want to talk much about his experiences. He was more interested in what was left of the farm and what they had to work with. He didn't know what he could do. The freed slaves would be leaving, and he wasn't strong enough to do much work. He had been shot in the leg, and it was broken. He had splinted it with a piece of board and continued fighting. It hadn't healed correctly. He was too tired to talk with the slaves about their future. He needed a hot bath, some food, and a good night's sleep before approaching them.

Hester was worried. "Now the war over, Marse Parrott be lettin' us go. I doesn't know what to do. Doesn't know nobody." Hester couldn't sleep that night. She was happy the Yankees didn't damage Mr. and Mrs. Parrott's bed, just hers.

They had dumped the goose down from her mattress. Every time she put a handful back into her mattress cover, the others floated all over the room. It looked like a winter snow. By the time she had them in the mattress and sewed it up again, goose feathers were all over her. Her bed wasn't as comfortable as it had been, but she was thankful she had that much left. Sitting by her window as the sun came up, she looked out over the plantation.

The Yankee soldiers who didn't come to the Great House had ridden their horses across the fields to ruin the crops. Mr. Parrott said Sherman's army of Yankees fought in a number of bloody campaigns. As they marched from Atlanta to the sea and then north into the Carolinas, where Hester lived, they meant to destroy the South.

The slaves were confused and worried. What would they do? They had nothing to take with them except what they wore. Winter was coming. Where would they get warm clothes? There was much to think and worry about with this "freedom thing."

Mr. Parrott felt he could not get out of bed. He ached all over and was very tired. He had so much on his mind. Most of what he had acquired was gone. He felt helpless. What can I do for my precious wife and family?

The household at least had warm milk for breakfast. Hester

thought, "Dis sho' diff'rent from de first breakfast I et here. Dem purty yellow walls, white curtains is gone. Ain't no purty flowers on the table. De silverware and dishes all bent up, broken. I wishes dem Yankees had stayed where dey comes from."

Mr. Parrott sent Hester to the slave quarters to round up all the slaves and bring them to the Great House. They walked up slowly, not knowing what to expect, gathered around in the yard facing the porch. Mr. Parrott stood for a few minutes looking at the men, women, and children in front of him. Their faces displayed some happiness they would be free, some sadness at not knowing what the future held. Mr. Parrott greeted them and told them he was happy to be home and thanked them for taking care of things the best they could while he was gone. "You are free. You are no longer my slaves. I don't know what you will do. As you know, I have nothing to give you because what I had is gone. I will be like you and will have to make a new start in life. I want you to know you are welcome to stay in your quarters until you find some place to go. You will have to find what you eat because we have nothing here. I hope you will remember me as a good master. I haven't had to punish any of you severely. You have worked obediently for me, and I appreciate it. You may come and talk to me any time and discuss what your plans are."

The slaves went back to their quarters without saying a word.

Slowly, Mr. Parrott walked into the house and slouched in his big chair as though he had the weight of the world on his shoulders. Closing his eyes, he sat quietly. In a few minutes, he felt the presence of someone nearby. Opening his eyes, he saw tiny Hester standing in front of him, tears running down her cheeks. Hester had to be somewhere around twenty years old, but she was so frail she didn't look her age. Mr. Parrott sat up straight and asked, "Hester is there something you want to talk to me about?"

"Yassuh, Marse Parrott. I jest doesn't know what I's goin' do. I ain't got nobody but you an yo family. I ain't got no Ma or Pa, an I don't know nobody 'cepting you folks here. What is I gone do, Marse Parrott? You is all de family I's got. I loves Missy Mary. I doesn't want to leave her. I ain't got no home to go to. I ain't got no money. I ain't got nothin'. Please, Marse Parrott, can't I stays here wit you an yo famly? I promises I will do all I can to help git things back in order agin."

"Come here, Hester. Taking her hands in his, he said, "You may stay here as long as you want. I know Mary will like having you here. She needs you."

Hester sobbed with relief. When she had recovered, she said, "I thanks you, Marse Parrott."

Chapter 17
Families Together

Hearing a knock at the door, Hester opened it to find a young boy with a note in his hand. "Kin I helps you?"

"Yas'um, I's got a paper fo Missy Mary Parrott. Will you gives it to her?"

"I sho' will," Hester said, as she took the note. Walking to the library to find Mary, she put the envelope to her nose and took a deep breath. The lavender fragrance crept into her nostrils.

"Missy Mary, I's got a note fo you, an it smell heavenly. Must be good news."

"Oh wonderful, Hester! Maybe it's from Brad." Mary hurriedly opened the letter. Inside she found the following:

My Dear Mary,

I know you and Brad were close, and that is why I am writing to you. I know you will be as hurt as his father and I are to learn that Brad was killed in battle. We are proud he fought for what he believed in but are heartbroken we will never see him again. I hope you will keep fond memories of him.

Love,

Mrs. Perkins

Mary clutched the letter to her heart and fell to the floor. Hester dropped to her knees beside her. Putting her hand on her shoulder and shaking her, she shouted, "Missy Mary, Missy Mary, is you alright?" Her heart was pounding. "Oh lordy, Missy Mary can't be dead! Missus Parrott, come quick! Something happen to Missy Mary!"

Mrs. Parrott came running in. "What happened, Hester? Get me some water. Quick!"

Hester ran into her room and came back with a pitcher of water and a bath cloth. Water was dripping from her dress where it had splashed from the pitcher as she came running down the stairs.

Mrs. Parrot placed the cool bath cloth on Mary's forehead.

Mary opened her eyes and immediately became hysterical.

"What is wrong, Mary?"

Mary would not answer. Hester picked the note up from the floor and handed it to Mrs. Parrott.

"Oh no! Hester, please get Mr. Parrott."

Mr. Parrott, rushing into the room, was shocked at what he saw. His wife handed him the note from Mrs. Perkins, took Mary in her arms, and held her tight.

Hester, standing by, knowing Missy Mary was heartbroken, said, "Missy Mary, everything will be alright. You'll see."

The Parrotts wished to express their sympathy, and a miracle let them. A hog that had been living deep in the swamp came wandering into the back yard. They sent a note to the Perkins inviting them to a barbecue dinner and killed, dressed, and cooked the animal over a pit of hot coals. The aroma drifted over the yard and into the house. It had been a long time since Hester had smelled anything cooking at the plantation. She was tempted to sneak out, pull off a chunk and eat it but decided against it.

"I wonders what we kin have wit de barbecue?" Then she remembered the cabbage kraut in the cellar and filled a large bowl with it. It wouldn't be as good as slaw, but it would have to do. Could there possibly be some cornmeal for cornbread? "Sarah, did you hide some cornmeal youse forgot?"

Sarah remembered she had put some in the attic under loose boards when she heard the Yankees were coming. Maybe it hadn't been found. Hester ran to the attic and, sure enough, the cornmeal was there. They had the cow, so bread could be made with buttermilk.[18] Things were coming together. "I wonders what we has fo dessert? I remembers seein' a bee hive down in de woods. If Roscoe can get us some honey, we kin et it on cornbread. We gots sweet taters, kin make candied yams with dat honey. Our stomachs ain't goin' to be turnin' an hurtin' from hunger fo a little while."

Roscoe wasn't happy but went into the woods in search of the beehive and its honeycomb. The bees were swarming. He reached in the hive, got out honey and honeycomb, and put them in the wooden bucket. The angry bees swarmed him, stinging him on his face and ears. He wasn't a pretty sight when he got back to the Great House. His ears were swollen twice their size, and his nose was so large his eyes were almost closed. Hester chewed some "medicinal" tobacco until it was soft and wet and

---

[18]To make buttermilk, soured milk was put in a large crock with a dasher (a wooden stick with paddles on the bottom). The dasher was pushed up and down until the cream turned into butter. What was left was buttermilk.

placed it on his face to help draw the pain from the stings.

Late afternoon the guests began arriving. Hester thought, "Dis ain't de invitin' home it be before, but it don't matter 'cause de neighbor folk gots Massa Devastation jist like usins. It good dey kin all be together an spend time wit Missy Mary. She sad but happy havin' Mistah Brad's parents here."

As Hester served the food, Mr. and Mrs. Parrott and Mr. and Mrs. Perkins spent a while discussing their situation and how to deal with it. They decided to help each other and make the load lighter.

Mary let the Perkins know how sorry she was for Brad's death.

After everyone left, Hester saw Mr. Parrott sitting in his big chair, pondering what he should do next.

"Mr. Parrott, does you need anything?"

"Hester, I think the first thing I'll do is plant a garden. That will give us food. There is a lot of work to be done. The apple and peach trees are still here, but they need pruning and fertilizing."

Hester was happy to see Mr. Parrott making plans and happy she could stay with his family. She would take care of Mary and do all she could to help with the garden and farm work.

Hester

Chapter 18

Hard Work to Be Done

"Roscoe, Marse John want you to go to town to git some seeds an supplies so we can plant us a garden. Marse John in de library. You go finds out what he need."

"I'll go right now, Hester." Roscoe was dedicated to the Parrott family and had decided to stay for a while to help them get their lives back together. He had a family but no home or anything to start a new life in the "freedom days." Mr. Parrott gave him permission to live where he was. Together, they could produce food for both families, and Roscoe's wife could do the washing. He found Mr. Parrott in the library and got the list of items to give to the store clerk. Roscoe couldn't read. He hooked the horse up to the buggy and left for town.

Hester felt sorry for Mrs. Parrott. Her beautiful dishes and goblets were broken. Not much silverware was left. For the first time in her life, she had to work with her hands and didn't know how.

On the way upstairs to check on whether any portraits were salvageable, Hester thought about the day she came to the Parrotts some ten years earlier. "Things sho' ain't the same today." Midway upstairs, she looked over the banister railing. The beautiful chandelier was still there, but the mirror that had reflected the rose-colored loveseat on the stairway wall was broken, and the seat was slashed to pieces. "I wonders how them soldiers woulda felt ifen somebody done dis to dere home." At the top of the stairs, as she looked down the hall, she saw no vases of fresh flowers on the tables. She would pick some and make everyone feel better. Carefully lifting the portraits from the broken frames, Hester carried them downstairs and put them on the dining room table. Missy Mary and Mrs. Parrott, after looking at them, decided some could be salvaged but wouldn't be as before.

The children's bedrooms seemed to be all right, except for the dresser drawers emptied on the floor by the soldiers looking for things of value. She already knew about Mary's room.

"I wonders if the pinano messed up?" Running down the stairs to the parlor, Hester was relieved to find it still there. She held her breath as she opened the lid and began pressing each key. The best she could tell, they sounded as before. It was good Martha wasn't there to tell her to leave that "pinano" alone. She hoped Mrs. Parrott would play some more beautiful songs on it.

Mr. Parrott had been assessing the outside. The big barn was burned to the ground, along with the smoke house where they stored meat and molasses. He and Roscoe could cut down trees for a log building and make a shed for the animals. The yellow fever he'd caught in the war had left him very thin and undernourished. There was little food except for the birds, rabbits, and squirrels Roscoe killed and the fish he caught from the stream near the house. They still had some sweet potatoes. One of the hens laid eggs and had set on them until chicks were hatched.

With an ox hitched to the plow, Mr. Parrott hobbled out to begin plowing up a plot for a garden. After breaking the land up, he used a different plow point to ridge the rows. When Roscoe got back, Hester walked along them dropping little seeds in holes made on the tops of the rows. They planted field peas, butter beans, corn, and green beans. It was too late for garden peas, cabbage, and turnips, which liked cooler weather. They did put out some onion sets that had to be placed almost on top of the ground and some white and red potatoes. After they finished planting, Mr. Parrott prayed, "Lord, please bless this garden that it may grow and give us food."

"Marse John, I jist believes mighten be some tobacco seed in dat tobacco field. I knows de Yankee soldiers rode up and down dem tobacco rows and broke down de tobacco stalks. Ise gone take a little sack an git Roscoe's Lou to go wid me. She know more 'bouts it dan I does."

Hester stopped at Roscoe's cabin, and Lou agreed to help. They walked out into the field. "Hester, when 'bacca grow up big, jist afore time to crop hit an put hit in de barn, big bunches dese flowers grows in de top of de plant. Dey gots to be broke off, else dey tak de strength from de plant. Dem Yankee soldiers ain't knowin' how important it be to leave flowers in de tops of 'bacca plants, so maybe dey ain't destroy dem all. De seeds comes from dem flowers. We see if some left."

"Lou, looks! I believes I sees some flowers dat looks 'most dead." Running over to the plant, Hester picked up a stalk and held it over her palm. Tiny seeds fell out. "Come quick, Lou. I's found some! Jist look! Dere a lot of plants wit seeds. Enough to plant a big crop for us and Marse Perkins. Ain't dat something, Lou? I knows Marse Parrott be happy. Let's put dem seeds in dis bag and go tells him."

Hester ran so fast across the tobacco field Lou couldn't keep up. Arriving at the house, she called Mr. Parrott, who, afraid something else was wrong, came quickly out on the back porch. "Dere ain't nothin' wrong, Marse Parrott. I's got de best news ever. Jist look at dese 'bacca seeds Lou an me finds. Enough for us an Marse Perkins. Ain't dat good news?"

"How in the world did you find so many seeds, Hester?"

"Well, Lou tells me how some flowers left on a few plants to make seeds. We knowed dem Yankee soldiers ain't know nothing 'bout growing tobacco, so we believes we kin find some what had seeds, and you kin see we did. Ain't dat great, Marse Parrott?"

"That is the best news I have heard since I got home, Hester. You may have just saved us from losing our farm and home. Thank you so much. And thank you too, Lou. I am happy you chose to stay with us. You have been a big help."

Hester

Chapter 19

A Big Decision for Hester

Hearing a knock on the back door, Hester took her hands from the dishwater, dried them on her apron, and opened it to find what appeared to be an old woman. "Kin I helps you, Ma'am?"

"I's been told dere a slave girl here name of Hester. Be she here?"

"Yasam, I Hester. I lives here."

"Yo ma name Carol?"

"Yasam, my ma Carol, my pa Sainty, an I had a baby brother name o' William. Ma die, an I ain't see my pa or brother since I sold when I five years old. How you know my ma?"

"I Carol's ma. You is my grandchild. I's been looking everwhere fo you. I heered Carol had a girl name Hester but didn't know where you was. I kept looking an asking an finally I talked wit a slave woman tole me a girl workin' fo de Parrotts name Hester. Dat how I fines you."

Hester stared at the strange woman. Doubt crept into her mind. How could she have a grandmother after all this time? "Is you sure you my grandma?"

"Yes, I sure, Hester."

"Oh lordy! Oh lordy! Missus Eliza, Missy Mary, everbody come here!" Hester was running around in circles, clapping her hands and shaking her head as if she was having a fit.

Mrs. Eliza and Mary came rushing to see what was wrong. Hester was acting strange, like a chicken when Sarah chopped its head off. They saw an elderly Negro woman standing by the table. Sprigs of grey hair peeped from under her bonnet, and her calico dress looked new. She appeared rather tired. Mrs. Parrott was surprised to see her so well dressed and wondered who she was and where she came from.

Hester was wringing her hands and crying. "Look who's here! Look who's here!" She was taking long steps and clapping her hands. She stood up, then repeated the action. Had she lost her mind? They had never seen Hester so shaken. "What is wrong, Hester?"

"Ain't nothing wrong, Missus Eliza. This here my grandma. She is done found me! I is got some family after all." Suddenly

Hester realized it was true. She did have family. She ran to her grandmother, who took her in her arms. Hester sobbed as she had when her mother died. She never even bothered to ask her name. It didn't matter to her. Names, especially last names, had never had any meaning to her.

"Hester, I is yo grandma, and I's come to take you to my home in Magnolia to live wit me."

Hester had a big decision to make. Should she go with her grandmother or stay with the Parrotts? They were her family, too, and she loved them. She was upset and needed a little time. She ran out of the house and sat on the bench under the big oak tree. She had some thinking to do.

Mrs. Parrott and Hester's grandmother understood that Hester needed some time to herself. It was a shock for her to find out so suddenly she had family.

When Hester had herself together, she walked back into the house. Mrs. Parrott had made her grandmother a glass of tea, and they were chatting. Hester stood before Mrs. Parrott and, with tears running down her boney cheeks, said, "Missus Parrott, you knows dis a hard decision fo me. You knows I loves you and Missy Mary and Marse Parrott like family. You is de only family I's ever knowed. But *dis* my *true* famly. It hurt me all over to leave you, but I is got to go wit my grandma. Please ask Marse Parrott to join us in the library."

Once they were all there, Hester stood looking at them for a few minutes, tears flowing down her cheeks.

Mrs. Parrott explained to her husband what was happening.

"Marse Parrott, you knows how much I loves dis family. Missy Mary my best friend in de world. But I has a grandma now. All my life I has wanted a family. I thanks you fo lettin' me stay wit you when us slaves freed. I stay on wit you foever iffen my grandma ain't found me. I knows you understands I has to leave you."

"Yes, Hester, I do understand, and I am so happy you have family."

Hester went to Mary, took her in her arms, and they both cried. Mary was heartbroken. "Missy Mary, you knows I loves you better dan anything. You is like a sister to me. Will you promise we stay in touch wit each other and see each other as long as we live?"

"Yes, Hester, I surely will keep in touch with you always."

"Is I got to go wit you today, Grandma?"

"Yes, Hester. I ain't be able to come dis far agin to git you."

Mary and Hester walked hand-in-hand upstairs to gather

Hester's belongings. Hester looked in the mirror, knew she looked a lot different from when she first came there ten years before. She walked to the bed and ran her hands down the smooth quilt remembering the first time she slept in a real bed. She thought about the many nights she sat at the window pondering things and trying to sort them out in her mind. She had learned so much, like making up a feather bed, dusting, and setting a table. She remembered that first breakfast of ham, grits, eggs, biscuits, jelly, and milk. Oh, there were so many memories!

Mary took Hester by the hand and led her to her wardrobe. "Hester, you don't have to wear dark dresses anymore. I am going to give you some of mine. You and I are about the same size, so I'm sure you can wear them." She took several of her dresses from the wardrobe and placed them in a bag she handed to Hester.

"Missy Mary, you shouldn't give me dese dresses. Since de war, you ain't able to buy you no mo pretty dresses."

"That's all right, Hester. I don't need any pretty dresses. There isn't any place to go for parties, and, with Brad gone, it doesn't matter."

"Oh, thank you, thank you, Missy Mary. I's always wanted to wear a pretty dress since the time I first came here and you show me some of yours. You is so kind, and I loves you."

The two went back downstairs and joined the others. Hester got on the wagon with her grandma, and they began the journey to Hester's new home. Her emotions were mixed. She knew Missy Mary would soon find someone to love and marry, but she would have a new life also. "What a wonderful but sad day this has been," thought Hester. She never looked back as Grandma led the mule and wagon onto the main road.

Chapter 20

Hester's New Life in FREEDOM

The wheels of the wagon made a swishing sound as they turned in deep sandy ruts in the road. The mule swept its tail back and forth shooing the flies away. Other than these sounds, it was very quiet.

At last, Hester said, "Grandma, I's so happy you finds me. I just knowed I ain't had no family. Thank you fo keepin' on lookin' fo me. I felt I never have any family to love."

"Hester, child, in my heart I knowed I had to have a grandchild out there somewheres. I had to keep lookin'. It was a miracle I found somebody that knowed you and your ma."

"Grandma, it was terrible when Ma die. I was sad, and life terrible. Thank goodness Marse Parrott bought me and gave me to his girl, Mary. I loves her, Grandma, an I dreadin' leavin' her, but I knows we to keep on seein' each other. She promise me dat. Grandma, was you a slave?"

"Yes, Hester, I was, but dat all in de past. We not gone discuss it nomore. I knows we goin' to have a hard life rite on, but thank goodness, I has a little house we lives in, and I has a job in Magnolia. Good people dere."

The two rode in silence for a while, both thinking about the past and what the future held for them.

"Grandma, I believes I's been on dis road before. Dese white houses wit de peach and apple orchards spread across the field as far as you can see, dat pond wit de geese an ducks a-swimmin' on it, dem pigs rootin' in de mud, an dem cows eatin' grass in de pasture sure does look familiar."

Hester remembered traveling the road with Mr. Bishop, Mr. Miller, and Mr. Parrott. She also remembered going to a little town with Mrs. Parrott, Missy Mary, and Roscoe, but she didn't remember the name of it being "Magnolia." When she went, it was "Stricklandsville." She remembered seeing the slaves tied together and walking in hot sand that long, long trip. She remembered going to a little town and being put on the auction block and sold.

"Grandma, does you know a little town down dis road where slaves sold?"

"De town of Kenansville is where de slaves sold, Hester. We goin' right through dere."

"Oh my, Grandma, dat jist where I sold to Mr. Miller and Mr. Parrott. I was scairt. Mens staring at me on de auction block. I is so happy I don't have to do dat no mo."

When they rode into Kenansville, Hester had cold chills up and down her spine as she saw the familiar houses and the courthouse, but the auction block was no longer there. She was happy for that.

"Grandma, can I aks you somethin?"

"Of course you can, Hester. What is it?"

"Grandma, a spring of warter dere by de courthouse. Can we stop dere and git a drink o' cool warter?"

"Yes, Hester. Some warter taste mighty good." Grandma pulled on the lines and went to a hitching post. "Whoa, mule." When the mule stopped, she got down from the wagon, fastened the lines to the post, and said, "Come on, Hester."

They walked to the spring and down the steps. Hester cupped her hands and caught the water in them and drank as she did about ten years before. The water was cool and refreshing. Grandma stepped up to the flow of water and did the same. After they had plenty, they got on the wagon and continued their journey.

Hester and her grandmother were nearing the end of their trip. It was only about eight miles from Kenansville to Magnolia. Hester wondered where Grandma lived. "I bets it ain't no big fine house like the Parrotts', but dat's all right. Jist bein' wit my real family, I be happy."

In Magnolia, Hester saw Elm trees that reached from one side of the street to the other. Her grandmother finally stopped the mule at a small, gray-looking, unpainted house. She got down from the wagon, reached in to get Hester's belongings, and said, "Welcome to my home, Hester."

Hester sat staring for a few minutes. She had gotten used to the Parrotts' fine home, even though the Yankees had destroyed it. She thought, "Is I got to go back to livin' in a cabin agin?" But she soon found out that the little house had wooden floors, not dirt ones. In a corner stood a wood stove used for cooking, heating water, and warming the house in the winter. On another wall was a punched tin safe just like Bessie's and Josephine's. There was a crude table and benches, and two rocking chairs were placed on each side of the fireplace.

Two bedrooms were off the kitchen. In Hester's was an iron bed with a feather mattress, which was all right with her. She had learned to master that. She didn't have a wardrobe or dresser, so she hung the pretty dresses Mary had given her on nails driven into the wall. Soon she smelled something good. Her grandmother was cooking. She didn't realize how hungry she was. It had been a long trip, and the little bit of food they brought from the Parrotts' house had been gone long since.

When she entered the kitchen, Hester asked if she could help.

"Does you knows how to make biskits, Hester?"

"No ma'am, I's never done much cookin'. I mostly clean de house an look afta Missy Mary an de little childrens."

"Den you best be watchin' and learnin'. You is gonna have to cook someday, child. If you ever gets married, dat man will expect some good vittles."

Her grandmother was at the table mixing biscuits in a large wooden tray. Hester was amazed at how she could break off a bit of dough, pat it out, place it in a pan, and have all the biscuits the same size. She had a lot of learning to do. For supper, they had the biscuits, fat back meat, and molasses, with coffee to drink. It was brewed on the back of the stove and was strong enough to let you know it was coffee. All Hester had had before was like tinted water. After the long trip, even fat back meat tasted good. When the dishes were washed, they both felt very tired and were ready to go to sleep.

Passing by her grandmother's room to go to her own, Hester saw her on her knees by her bed, heard her thanking God for letting her find her grandchild. Hester went over, knelt beside her, and thanked Him for answering her and her grandmother's prayers. At last, just as she had always hoped and imagined, she had a blood-kin family to be with permanently and love.